Old Names and New Places

By
ROBERT I. ALOTTA

Illustrations by
LEE DeGROOT

THE WESTMINSTER PRESS
Philadelphia

Book Design by Dorothy Alden Smith

First edition

PUBLISHED BY THE WESTMINSTER PRESS ®
PHILADELPHIA, PENNSYLVANIA

PRINTED IN THE UNITED STATES OF AMERICA

9 8 7 6 5 4 3 2 1

Historic prints used in the illustrations are reproduced courtesy of the Print and Picture Department, The Free Library of Philadelphia.

COVER: *Delaware's oldest homestead and blockhouse*

Library of Congress Cataloging in Publication Data

Alotta, Robert I
  Old names and new places.

  Bibliography: p.
  Includes index.
  SUMMARY: Presents stories behind many place names in the United States and makes suggestions for going about such research.
  1. Names, Geographical—United States—Juvenile literature. 2. United States—History, Local—Juvenile literature. [1. Names, Geographical. 2. United States—History, Local] I. DeGroot Lee. II. Title
E155.A53   917.3'03   78–20915
ISBN 0–664–32647–1

To the night that never was

Contents

An Exchange of Names

Have you ever walked out your front door and looked at the street sign down by the corner and wondered why it carried that name and not some other name?

Or, while traveling across the countryside, have you ever been curious about a town or city with an unusual or strange-sounding name?

If you have, you are one of a rapidly growing group of Americans who are interested in knowing the story behind a name. Under the name of "folk history," this hobby is becoming a very popular pastime. It can take the "name detective" back into the early days of America, and you don't ever have to leave home, school, or library.

To investigate name origins, you don't need special skills, courses, or experience. All you really need is curiosity and a little direction.

The curiosity must be yours. The direction can be obtained by turning these pages.

There's a street in Philadelphia with the strange-sounding name of Wingohocking.

It is not the kind of name one would expect to find in any dictionary, let alone on a city street sign. Wingohocking is the type of name that makes a person ask who? what? and why?

Wingohocking was not the name of a place, nor was it the name of a thing. It was the name of a man, an Indian chief who lived in the wilds of Philadelphia during the seventeenth century.

The chief was very friendly with James Logan, colonial secretary under William Penn, the founder of Philadelphia. He spent many enjoyable hours at Logan's estate, "Stenton."

One day, while the two were standing by a stream that ran through Logan's property, Chief Wingohocking suggested that they show their undying affection and friendship for each other—in the tradition of the Indians. Wingohocking suggested that they exchange names!

Rather than offend his associate, Logan told him: "Do thou, chief, take mine, and give thine to this stream which passes through my fields, and when I am passed away and while the earth shall endure it shall flow and bear thy name."

The chief reluctantly accepted this modification of his gesture, and, as Logan predicted, the stream continued to flow through the fields of "Stenton" long after both men had ceased walking the pathways of this earth. In the nineteenth century, when city planners found it necessary to fill in the waterway and replace it with a street, Wingohocking's name was retained, perhaps in an unconscious effort to fulfill Logan's promise.

The chief's name is still alive today and the tale of that act of friendship will continue to be told as a reminder to future generations as long as that street exists.

The name Wingohocking cannot be found in any place but Philadelphia. However, other streets, other places and geographic features bear equally unique names and have equally fascinating stories.

Finding out why something bears the name it does can provide many hours of happy detective work. The results will provide the investigator with an entirely different perspective on history—a people-oriented account of what life was like before we arrived.

Strangers in the Land

When the first Europeans arrived on America's shores, they were strangers in the land of the American Indians, the native-born residents of the continent.

Like the Europeans, the Indians had names for the villages where they lived, the rivers that provided transportation and communication, and the hills and mountains where they hunted and foraged. But the Indians did not keep a written history. There were no records as to why they named something. Unlike their successors on the land, they did not erect signposts.

To the early American immigrants, the Indian names were foreign. Though they tried, the settlers were, for the most part, unable to master the vocabulary of the natives.

So they corrupted the Indian names into Dutch, Swedish, and English sounds. When a name was impossible to pronounce and couldn't be modified, the Europeans took the route of least resistance—they changed the name to one that was much more familiar to them.

Besides being easier to pronounce and spell, the altered names helped relieve a little of the immigrants' homesickness. The Europeans were thousands of miles away from home and family. They could not take a flight back home, or phone. The only way they could return to the land of their birth was in their dreams, or by long and hazardous voyages across the Atlantic Ocean.

It was quite natural—and human—for the settlers to miss their families and friends. They longed for the friendly faces, the familiar places, the hundred and one little things they remembered

from home. Because they had made the decision and the commitment to begin life anew in this unspoiled land, they had to bring some little remnant of their old existence to make this new existence more tolerable.

So, when settlers from Plymouth, England, landed on the rocky shores of the northern coast of America they called the area New England and their landing spot Plymouth. And when the Swedes sailed up the Delaware River and established their first settlement it was logical for them to call it New Sweden. Like the Indian names, New Sweden was not completely acceptable to the succeeding English colonists, so they changed the name to Wilmington. As usual, the stronger people took from the weaker.

Throughout the east coast of North America, the transplanted names of Europe took root. The familiar names made the colonists feel more comfortable.

But the familiar names of the homeland were not enough. This lush new land was different from the England, Sweden, and Holland they remembered. America was a wilderness. It had not been tamed by successive conquests as had Europe. No mixture of cultures had altered the face of the land and dictated the architecture.

The American continent was virgin territory. It was up to the immigrants to remake and name their homesteads in the image and likeness they could comprehend.

CHAPTER 3

Converting Old Names

Depending on your persuasion, the eastern coastline of America was first discovered by St. Brendan of Ireland, Leif Erickson of Norway, or Christopher Columbus of Italy, via Spain.

Regardless of which explorer first sighted the shores, the name was given to the continents by a man who had never even seen them.

Martin Waldseemüller, a German geographer, honored the Florentine navigator and explorer Amerigo Vespucci by bestowing his first name on the new land. He did this after translating Vespucci's accounts of his voyages along the coasts of Central and South America while in the service of Spain—shortly after Columbus' voyages.

Any modern Americans who have difficulty spelling complicated words and names should rejoice that Waldseemüller was a humble man and did not use his own name, and further, that he chose Vespucci's first name, not his second.

Because of a strong, almost all-consuming desire for worldwide possession, many of the European governments dispatched explorers and fortune seekers across the dangerous waters of the Atlantic Ocean to uncover the riches and wealth of the untouched New World. Spain was in the forefront.

It was fitting then that the first permanent settlement in the Americas was founded by the Spaniards in 1565. The colony, located in Florida, was named St. Augustine, out of a sense of religious thankfulness.

Not to be outdone by their enemies, the English followed in the footsteps of Spain. Arriving from London aboard the *Phoenix,* English settlers colonized the coast of Virginia, establishing a fort and village in 1607. This compound they called Jamestown, in honor of King James I, who permitted them to suffer the pain and anguish of colonization in the foreign land.

The Jamestown settlement was not too successful. In fact, a majority of the settlers died from disease and exposure to the elements. If they had not received word that help was on the way, they might have vacated the village entirely.

On August 27, 1610, Captain Samuel Argall anchored his vessel a short distance north of Jamestown in a bay which he quickly named "the De la Warre bay" in homage to his superior, Sir Thomas West, third Lord de la Warr. The name over the years has been altered to Delaware.

Unknown to Argall, his fellow countryman Henry Hudson had anchored in that same bay one year before to the month. Not having the wherewithal to explore further, Hudson sailed up the coast into another harbor and into a river that now bears his name.

The Dutch were busy too. They were settling to the north about the same time that the British were suffering in Virginia. They called their land, for obvious reasons, New Amsterdam. It wasn't a profitable colony, the Dutch West India Company learned. It drained their resources. So, by 1664, when the British took control the Dutch weren't unconsolable. Ten years later a royal charter was issued to James, Duke of York, brother of King Charles II. Because it was his new colony, the Duke of York thought it fitting to rename it New York.

The English were also active. In 1620, they arrived in Massachusetts and established another piece of homeland. They called their village Plymouth, after their hometown in England.

Many of the first settlers in the New World were individuals who were dissatisfied with the organization and ritual of the religion in their homeland and wanted to change it. Faced with strong criticism and personal and economic persecution, they found it most convenient to leave and to travel to more agreeable religious climates.

Some of these reformers were Puritans, members of the established Church of England. They desired to "purify" the church of its falseness and pretense. They wanted to return to the simple life of the early Christians. Others were Separatists. These individuals wanted to remove themselves from the church itself and start new, fresh—and separate—religions.

Regardless of the desire to improve or re-create their religions, these early reformers used the Bible as their primary reader. And, using the words found in the Old Testament—in Genesis, Exodus, Leviticus, Numbers, and Joshua—they found similarities between their flight from Europe and the exodus of the Jews from Egypt. This correspondence caused them to bestow Biblical names on their towns and villages, such as Bethel in Connecticut and Maine, and Jericho in Vermont.

But they could never forget the king of England! They were in this free land by his grace. This they could not ignore, and if they tried, His High Mightiness would have an emissary remind them.

The English kings, because of the reports of the early explorers, took it for granted that they were the legal owners of all of America. With that understanding, they gave out charters and grants to a chosen few, as presents for services rendered to the crown, or for a price.

Towns sprang up in New England, along the Charles River, which was named for King Charles I. One town was named Charlestown because they didn't want the king to think that one place name was adequate for a person of his high position. Others were Boston, Medford, Watertown, Rocksbury, Salem, and Dorchester, in the colony of Massachusetts.

They didn't change or convert all the old names. After all, the natives wouldn't stand for it—especially the Massachuset, Narragansett, Mohegan (Mohican), and other tribes. In many sections of New England, those names still remain as silent testimony to the American Indian.

Word of the reported success of these colonists spurred others.

George Calvert, Baron of Baltimore, in the Irish peerage and a recent convert to Catholicism, had a dream. He wanted to see a colony somewhere, anywhere, that could provide religious freedom for all people, especially Roman Catholics.

He first tried to implement his idea on a tract of land in Newfoundland, later patented to him by James I as the Province of Avalon. Calvert, however, soon was disgusted "with his intolerable plantation . . . where he hath found between eight and nine months of winter."

The Baron of Baltimore tried his luck farther south, just above the colony of Virginia, from 1626 to 1630. The climate and location suited him and he quickly decided to create a sister colony to Virginia on the Chesapeake Bay.

A charter was issued by Charles I on June 20, 1632—and assigned to Calvert's twenty-six-year-old son, Cecilius (Cecil), the second Lord Baltimore. Young Calvert named the new colony the Province of Maryland. Because of Calvert's religion, many people thought he named the province in honor of Mary, the mother of Christ. Perhaps in the back of his mind, that was his intention. On the surface, however, he announced that he was naming it after the wife of his king.

The entire state of Maryland carries the Calvert imprint. Counties, cities, and towns remind contemporaries of the contribution made by the family.

Back up in the north, more hardy settlers established a plantation in Connecticut at Quinnipiac. Finding that name too difficult to curl across their tongues, the English changed it to New Haven on September 1, 1640. But they did allow the river to keep the name, which is Quinnipiac on today's maps.

Two years later, the English bought land along the Schuylkill River in an area of the Delaware Valley known to the Indians as Wickquacoingh—another tongue twister—which was quickly contracted to Wicaco. That too was unmanageable and only a street in present-day Philadelphia bears the ancient name.

Progress was moving rapidly by this time. The Duke of York presented land to Sir John Berkeley and Sir George Carteret alongside his New York settlement. That land was called Nova Caesarea, which became in English "New Jersey."

In 1681, King Charles II presented a charter to young William Penn for a vast portion of the New World. The king, though quite friendly with Penn's father, was embarrassed by William's staunch

NEWFOUNDLAND

SIR GEO. CALVERT (LORD BALTIMORE).

MARYLAND

adherence to a new religion, a nondenomination—The Society of Friends, known also as Quakers because the members were known to shiver and shake *only* in the presence of God, not man.

Penn took the king's grant and sent his emissaries to Pennsylvania. Contrary to local tradition, the province was not named after him.

William Penn's original name for the granted territory was New Wales. But, on March 14, 1681, when King Charles signed the charter, the name was given as "Pennsilvania."

Embarrassed that someone might consider such a name as un-Friendly egotism, Penn explained to his friend Robert Turner that the name was given "in honor of my father . . . but Penn being Welsh for *a head,* [they] called this Pennsylvania, which is the high or head woodlands; for I proposed, when the secretary, a Welshman, refused to have it called New Wales, *Sylvania,* and they added *Penn* to it; and though I much opposed it, and went to the king to have it struck out and altered, he said it was past, and would take it upon him; nor could twenty guineas move the undersecretary to vary the name; for I feared lest it should be looked on as vanity in me, and not as a respect in the kind, as it truly was, to my father, whome he often mentions with praise."

Penn set up his province, his "virgin settlement," into six counties: Buckingham, Chester, New Castle, Kent, Sussex, and Philadelphia. The first five he named for places in England. The last, Philadelphia, was a created word of Greek origin. Wanting to use this city and county as the center of his development, Penn desired to have it, by its very name, connote the true meaning of his religion. Thus, "Philadelphia" translates to "city of brotherly love."

William Penn did more than just name his counties; he also named his streets according to a master plan—something that many early town planners did not do.

In his *Further Account of Pennsylvania,* published in 1685, the Founding Father wrote: "Besides Broad Street, which crosseth the town in the middle . . . there are twenty streets more, that run the same course and area also fifty feet broad. The names of those streets are mostly taken from the things that grow spontaneously in the country, as Vine Street, Mulberry Street, Chestnut Street, Walnut Street, Strawberry Street, Cranberry Street, Plum Street, Hickory Street, Pine Street, Oak Street, Beech Street, Ash Street, Poplar Street, Sassafras Street, and the like." Ironically, the majority of the named streets in Penn's original plan still carry the names given them, though the living things for which they were named have long since disappeared from the area.

Penn's chronicles are among the few that are available to researchers and other interested persons who want to learn the reasoning behind the naming of towns and streets. Too often, the namers are confident that contemporaries are aware of the reasons, but give little thought to making a permanent record so future generations will know.

A reason for the propensity for English-sounding names in Penn's territory is given in another section of his *Account:* "The people are a collection of divers nations in Europe: as, French, Dutch, Germans, Swedes, Danes, Finns, Scots, Irish, and English: and of the last equal to all the rest."

But these other ethnic groups were not content to be left out in the naming game. They made their mark on settlements of their own, such as the German villages at Gettysburg in Pennsylvania, and Hagerstown in Maryland, and in the Moravian settlements of Bethlehem, Nazareth, and Lititz, in Pennsylvania. The French named a mountain range. When they viewed the territory and found it to be a hilly midland, it made sense to them to call it Piedmont, which in their native tongue meant "foot of the mountain."

Every person who explored or settled the new land tried to make his mark by naming a river, a town, or a mountain after himself or after someone with whom he could curry favor. Everyone wanted to succeed and be forever remembered.

Human nature hasn't changed much since those days.

Devoutly Religious

Though early settlers to the American shores were devoutly religious, the majority were not showy about it—at least not on the East Coast.

As we've seen, the Protestant colonists commemorated their hometowns in the naming of their new towns. It was up to the Spanish and French pioneers, many Roman Catholic, to leave religious names on the land.

They used *saint* and *sainte* (French masculine and feminine), *san* and *santa* (Spanish masculine and feminine)—words meaning "saint" or "holy." They hoped that the dedication of a town to a religious figure would impart blessings on their endeavors.

A sampling of these names includes:

ALABAMA: Saint Bernard, Saint Clair, Saint Elmo, Saint Stephens
ALASKA: Saint Marys, Saint Michael, Saint Paul Island
ARIZONA: Saint David, Saint Johns, Saint Michaels, San Carlos, San Luis, San Manuel, San Simon
ARKANSAS: Saint Charles, Saint Francis, Saint James, Saint Joe, Saint Paul
CALIFORNIA: Saint Helena, Saint Mary's College, San Andreas, San Anselmo, San Ardo, San Bernardino, San Bruno, San Carlos, San Clemente, San Diego, San Dimas, San Fernando, San Francisco, San Gabriel, San Geronimo, San Gregorio, San Jacinto, San Joaquin, San Jose, San Juan Bautista, San Juan Capistrano, San Leandro, San Lorenzo, San Lucas, San Luis Obispo, San Luis Rey, San Marcos, San Martin, San Mateo, San Miguel, San Pedro,

San Quentin, San Rafael, San Ramon, San Simeon, Santa Clara, San Ysidro

COLORADO: San Acacio, San Luis, San Pablo

DELAWARE: Saint Georges

FLORIDA: Saint Augustine, Saint Catherine, Saint Cloud, Saint James City, Saint Leo, Saint Marks, Saint Petersburg, San Antonio, San Mateo

GEORGIA: Saint George, Saint Marys

IDAHO: Saint Anthony, Saint Charles, Saint Maries

ILLINOIS: Saint Anne, Saint Augustine, Saint Charles, Saint David, Saint Elmo, Sainte Marie, Saint Francisville, Saint Jacob, Saint Joseph, Saint Libory, Saint Peter, San Jose

INDIANA: Saint Anthony, Saint Bernice, Saint Croix, Saint Joe, Saint John, St. Louis Crossing, St. Mary of the Woods, St. Meinrad, Saint Paul, San Pierre, Santa Claus

IOWA: Saint Ansgar, Saint Anthony, Saint Charles, Saint Donatus, Saint Lucas, Saint Marys, and Saint Olaf

KANSAS: Saint Francis, Saint George, Saint John, Saint Marys, Saint Paul

KENTUCKY: Saint Catharine, Saint Charles, Saint Francis, Saint Helens, Saint John, Saint Joseph, Saint Mary, Saint Paul, Saint Vincent

LOUISIANA: Saint Amant, Saint Benedict, Saint Bernard, Saint Francisville, Saint Gabriel, Saint James, Saint Joseph, Saint Landry, Saint Martinville, Saint Maurice, Saint Rose

MAINE: Saint Agatha, Saint Albans, Saint David, Saint Francis, Saint George

MARYLAND: Saint George Island, Saint Inigoes, Saint James, Saint Leonard, Saint Marys City, Saint Michaels

MICHIGAN: Saint Charles, St. Clair, Saint Clair Shores, Saint Helen, Saint Ignace, Saint James, Saint Johns, Saint Joseph, Saint Louis, Sault Sainte Marie

MINNESOTA: Saint Bonifacius, Saint Charles, Saint Clair, Saint Cloud, Saint Francis, Saint Hilaire, Saint James, Saint Joseph, Saint Leo, Saint Martin, Saint Michael, Saint Paul, Saint Paul Park, Saint Peter, Saint Vincent

MISSISSIPPI: Bay Saint Louis

MISSOURI: Saint Albans, Saint Ann, Saint Catharine, Saint Charles, Saint Clair, Sainte Genevieve, Saint Elizabeth, Saint James, Saint Joseph, Saint Louis, Saint Marys, Saint Patrick, Saint Peters, Saint Thomas

MONTANA: Saint Ignatius, Saint Regis, Saint Xavier

NEBRASKA: Saint Columbans, Saint Edward, Saint Helena, Saint Libory, Saint Mary, Saint Paul

NEW MEXICO: Saint Vrain, San Acacia, San Antonio, San Cristobal, San Fidel, San Jon, San Jose, San Juan Pueblo, San Patricio, San Rafael, San Ysidro

NEW YORK: Saint Bonaventure, Saint James, Saint Johnsville, Saint Josephs, Saint Regis Falls

NORTH CAROLINA: Saint Pauls

NORTH DAKOTA: Saint Anthony, Saint John, Saint Michael, Saint Thomas, San Haven

OHIO: Saint Henry, Saint Johns, Saint Louisville, Saint Martin, Saint Marys, Saint Paris

OKLAHOMA: Saint Louis

OREGON: Saint Benedict, Saint Helens, Saint Paul

PENNSYLVANIA: Saint Benedict, Saint Boniface, Saint Charles, Saint Clair, Saint Johns, Saint Marys, Saint Michael, Saint Peters, Saint Petersburg, Saint Thomas

PUERTO RICO: Saint Just, San Antonio, San German, San Juan, San Lorenzo, San Sebastian

SOUTH CAROLINA: Saint Charles, Saint George, Saint Matthews, Saint Stephen

SOUTH DAKOTA: Saint Charles, Saint Francis, Saint Lawrence, Saint Onge

TENNESSEE: Saint Andrews, Saint Bethlehem, Saint Joseph

TEXAS: Saint Hedwig, Saint Joe, San Angelo, San Antonio, San Augustine, San Benito, San Diego, San Elizario, San Felipe, San Isidro, San Jacinto Monument, San Juan, San Marcos, San Perlita, San Saba, San Ygnacio

UTAH: St. George, Saint John

VERMONT: Saint Albans, Saint Albans Bay, Saint Johnsbury, Saint Johnsbury Center

VIRGINIA: Saint Charles, Saint David's Church, Saint Paul, Saint

Stephens Church
WASHINGTON: Saint John
WEST VIRGINIA: Saint Albans, Saint George, Saint Marys
WISCONSIN: Saint Cloud, Saint Croix Falls, Saint Germain, Saint
  Nazianz
WYOMING: Saint Stephens

Not all these holy cities are, in fact, named for recognized religious personalities. To cite a few examples, Saint Louis, Missouri, was founded by loyal Frenchmen and named for King Louis IX. Saint Joe, Texas, commemorates Joe Howell. Originally it was called Joe, but townspeople took offense at such an insignificantly short name. Both Saint John and St. George, Utah, honor prominent Mormons—John Roseberry and George A. Smith. Saint Thomas, Pennsylvania, was first known as Campbellstown, named for Thomas Campbell. Saint Edward, Nebraska, commemorates a priest, Edward Serrels.

The original place namers must have enjoyed themselves when they set out to devise the names for their towns. Perhaps they chuckled to themselves, realizing that future generations would have difficulty separating legitimacy from legend.

Convenient Paths

When the first Europeans touched foot on the shoreline of the New World and tentatively explored the interior, they found that the native Americans had long walked and run through its forests and plains. It was important for the Indians to keep these pathways open for communication and trade, and for avenues to fish and hunt game.

The most important paths were beaten down by the moccasined feet into unseen, unmarked roadways—just wide enough for the passage of a single person.

With the advent of the European colonists, the need for communication, trade, and travel increased. The narrow Indian trails were widened and expanded under the thick soles of the settlers.

In the settlements, it was convenient to lay out a plan locating the houses, churches, meetinghouses, stores, and mills. But no effort was made to clear the way first. The constant, repeated traffic back and forth from place to place did what man was not yet ready to do.

Those who settled outside the confines of the urban community wanted privacy, but, at the same time, they did not want to be left out of the social and commercial life. They wanted to attend worship, sell their wares, and visit with family and friends. At first, they followed the Indian trails, but as the need for travel intensified, the pathways became roads, highways, and, later, turnpikes.

Though all the descriptive terms for pathways seem to communicate the same idea—a way of passage—they are not the same.

The smallest is an alley, a narrow back street. The word is derived from the old French *alee,* "a walk." A road, on the other hand, is a long, narrow stretch with a smoothed or paved surface. "Road" comes from an Old English word that meant "to ride." In other words, a road was designed to carry something—riders, carriages, and, later, motorized vehicles.

A street, so called from the Latin word *stratum,* is a layered length in a village, town, or city. It is a public thoroughfare, while a road or an alley might be restricted to private use only.

The next largest conveyance route is the avenue, which is a main street wider than any of the smaller ways. Classically, an avenue was a tree-lined road or driveway through the grounds of a country house or a building of great proportions. The word "avenue" comes from the French word *avenir,* "to approach."

A boulevard is a broad avenue in a city. It should not be found in a hamlet, village, or town. Sometimes, however, it is. Usually, a boulevard has a parklike appearance, with areas to the sides or center for the planting of trees, grass, or flowers. A parkway can be just as wide, but it should have a dividing strip and/or side strips for planting.

A highway is not confined to any one city, town, or village. It is a major artery that connects two places of importance. The name suggests that the roadway is more elevated than the surrounding countryside. A turnpike can resemble a highway in all regards but one: a turnpike is maintained by the levying of tolls. In the early days of this nation, barriers—tollgates—were set up across the highways at various spots to halt the passage of a vehicle until the fee was paid. The name is obtained from the Middle English word *turnepike,* a revolving barrier with spikes on it.

Having knowledge of all these terms did not mean that the colonists applied them properly. They had grandiose plans for their new homes and country and would not be constrained by mere definitions. If it sounded better to add "road" to a name than "highway," they would do it—it was the American way.

In our fiftieth state, Hawaii, the paths of the native Polynesians were also trodden and paved into roads, and often the native

names were kept. Ala Moana in Honolulu, for instance, means "Road Beside the Sea" and that's just what it is. On it one of the most famous shopping centers in the world has taken the same name.

Plotting a Name

Now the colonists began to do something with the land they had obtained through grant or purchase.

William Penn was far ahead of his time when he instructed his surveyor general, Thomas Holme, to develop a comprehensive plan for Philadelphia.

Holme developed a unique plan. He laid out a grid. Everything connected with his "grid plan" was symmetrical. The surveyor could have drafted his design for Philadelphia with nothing more than a straight-edged ruler and a sharp quill pen. One set of his streets traveled north and south, the other east and west. He allowed equal distances between all streets and suitable space in several sectors for parks and greenlands. While others, in their haste to get started, built before they planned, Holme developed his concept and then let the people proceed according to the plan. It was a simple idea, so simple that no one had ever thought of it.

Like all major innovations, Holme's plan took hold of the emerging nation's imagination and was "borrowed" by other engineers and planners. In fact, when new cities are contemplated today, Holme's "grid" is referred to and studied, and put into use.

But Philadelphia was not the first city to have a regular system for street-naming. New Amsterdam—now New York City—holds that honor. In the *Possession Book* of 1645, listings can be found for "Sudbury" and "Springer" as two established street names. Those, however, were the only ones. Others were referred to as "the twenty-four-foot-wide passageway leading from the store of Mr. So-and-So to the house of Mr. Not-Yet."

Philadelphia took the lead in street-naming and moved ahead with it. Holme originally wanted to commemorate all of Penn's friends and acquaintances. But the founder would not hear of such sacrilege. He instructed the surveyor to use only names that were unique to the area. So, the original Philadelphia streets were named for trees, bushes, and shrubs on the east-west axis; the north-south streets bore numbers. This technique has been duplicated in countless major—and minor—cities throughout this nation.

The colonists, however, did not want to be completely restricted. Being a hardy lot, they wanted to attach something of themselves to the streets and roads they had cleared. In the beginning, when more important things, like survival, concerned them, they would follow the grid pattern.

The chief street of any English-founded community was called "High," because it was important. By the time streets were generally named, "high" meant a built-up way or a road along a ridge. When the settlers had more than one street upon which to travel, they referred to the most frequently used one as the "main street." Later, the name would become officially Main Street and emerge as the symbol of Smalltown, U.S.A. High Street would disappear in all but a few cities.

Something else they had to consider was the relative location of a roadway. They were constructing schools, churches, meeting-houses, mills, courthouses, and bridges. Any road or street that led to one of these structures ultimately assumed the name of the destination: School House Lane; Church Road; Meeting House Lane; Mill Street; Court House Road; Bridge Street. Even the place to which the farmers brought their produce to sell took its name from its business: Market Street. And, when business prospered and grew and another market was established, they called it New Market Street.

Thoroughfares leading to other towns, villages, and cities also took on the name of the destination, such as the Bethlehem [Turn]Pike, Lancaster Road, Haverford Road, Baltimore [Turn]-Pike, the Richmond Road.

The colonists, before the American Revolution, also felt a cer-

tain obligation to remember their native heritage and the leaders of their homelands. They used titles of nobility and names of royal houses for streets, roads, and alleys: King, Queen, Prince, Princess, Duke, Crown, Hanover, Orange. Streets were given the first names of the members of the royal families: William, Edward, George, Charlotte, Sophia. During and immediately following the war, these names toppled, much as the concept of rule from afar toppled.

Americans now had new names with which to label their roadways. They selected the names of Greek and Roman heroes of Republican triumph, and they had an almost unending supply from their own men and women who helped make this land the "home of the free."

The rebels did not change everything. They retained the names of those who, even on English soil, continued to support their cause. And they could not forget the rivers and lakes that were so important to their everyday life.

The rivers provided them with drinking water, fish, and a means of travel from one settlement to another. The cities and towns that sprang up beside these waterways usually started on a street that bordered the water. Rather than call it "First Street," they selected "Front Street." In cities that were lucky enough to have the resources of two rivers, there were two Front Streets. Philadelphia was one such city, built between two rivers. To differentiate between the Front Streets, Philadelphians labeled one Delaware Front, the other Schuylkill Front. Finally, in the middle of the nineteenth century, to avoid and eliminate all confusion, the name Schuylkill Front was removed and replaced with a number.

To build streets and roads, the colonists had to remove natural barriers, such as trees and rocks. With only the strength of their arms and legs to wrest these obstacles from the soil, they wanted succeeding generations to remember the sweat, blood, and tears that had provided future convenience. This they noted in their naming: Flat Rock Road, Forest Avenue, Black Oak Street.

When the engineering of roads meant traveling through someone's land, the settlers usually allowed the owner the privilege of having the thoroughfare named for his property, as in Woodland

Avenue and Torresdale, or for himself, as in Wharton Street and Macalester Street. This made the loss of personal property seem less distressing to the homeowner. He was now immortal . . . at least in name.

With the creation of streets, roads, and avenues, the aggressive settlers began to feel hemmed in. They needed to expand. The eastern cities seemed too small to them. They didn't like the feeling of confinement. So, as they had years before, they packed up their belongings and moved westward. They took with them the experiences of the settlements—and the familiar names.

Westward Ho!

The colonists had learned a lesson since they had first arrived in the New World: Wild animals and unfriendly Indians were a constant threat to their lives and property.

As the eastern seaboard became too congested, and the lure of lush, untouched territory enticed them, they left the security of the establishment and forged out on their own. In the West more than the East, Indian names were frequently used.

Each new settlement was required to fortify itself. Jamestown, Virginia, was not only the first English settlement in America, it' was also the first military post, established to protect the settlers and preserve their hard-earned property. In the earliest days of exploration, the settlers armed themselves and fought for what was theirs. But there is strength in numbers—and strength in having soldiers precede a pioneering effort.

Before homes and farms could be created, a rough fortress had to be built. Then under the watchful eye of the garrison and the protection of their "fort," the town could grow.

Many of these early military establishments have disappeared—only the names remain to remind us that armed force was needed to keep this nation free.

Here are some of the better-known military posts around which towns and cities developed. The list is by no means all-inclusive. Some, such as Fort Washington, Pennsylvania, grew up around a temporary installation. George Washington encamped there before wintering at Valley Forge. Fort Wayne, Indiana, was constructed following General Wayne's victory at Fallen Timbers.

ALABAMA: Forts Davis, Deposit, Mitchell, Payne
ALASKA: Fort Yukon
ARIZONA: Forts Apache, Defiance, Huachuca,* Thomas
ARKANSAS: Fort Smith
CALIFORNIA: Forts Bidwell, Bragg, Dick, Jones, Sutter
COLORADO: Forts Collins, Garland, Logan, Lupton, Lyon, Morgan
FLORIDA: Forts Lauderdale, McCoy, Meade, Myers, Ogden,
  Pierce, White
GEORGIA: Forts Gaines, Screvan
HAWAII: Fort Shafter
INDIANA: Forts Branch, Ritner, Wagner, Wayne
IOWA: Forts Atkinson, Dodge, Madison
KANSAS: Forts Dodge, Leavenworth,* Scott
KENTUCKY: Forts Campbell,* Knox*
LOUISIANA: Fort Necessity
MAINE: Forts Fairfield, Kent
MARYLAND: Forts George G. Meade,* Howard
MINNESOTA: Fort Ripley
MISSISSIPPI: Fort Adams
MISSOURI: Fort Leonard Wood*
MONTANA: Forts Benton, Harrison, Peck, Shaw
NEBRASKA: Fort Calhoun
NEW JERSEY: Fort Lee
NEW MEXICO: Forts Bayard, Stanton, Sumner, Wingate
NEW YORK: Forts Ann, Covington, Edward, Hunter, Johnson,
  Miller, Montgomery, Plain
NORTH DAKOTA: Forts Clark, Ransom, Rice, Totten
OHIO: Forts Jennings, Laramie, Recovery, Seneca
OREGON: Forts Klamath, Rock
PENNSYLVANIA: Forts Loudon, Washington
SOUTH CAROLINA: Forts Lawn, Mill, Motte
SOUTH DAKOTA: Forts Meade, Pierre, Thompson
TEXAS: Forts Davis, Hancock, McKavett, Stockton, Worth
UTAH: Fort Duchesne
VIRGINIA: Forts Belvoir,* Blackmore, Defiance, Mitchell,
  Monroe*
WASHINGTON: Fort Steilacoom

WEST VIRGINIA: Forts Ashby, Gay, Seybert, Spring
WISCONSIN: Fort Atkinson
WYOMING: Forts Bridger, Fred Steele, Laramie, Washakie

Those listed with an asterisk (*) are still active military installations. The others are technically abandoned military posts around which communities have grown. Not all were developed primarily for the protection of the townspeople. Several were built for the defense of the entire country from enemy attack, whether from outside or from within.

As the settlers and pioneers forged new lives and communities for themselves, they carried with them the names they held dear.

ARLINGTON—This name was first used in Virginia about 1650 for the plantation of John Custis II. It was derived from the name of several English towns and also from the title of a prominent earl. It can now be found in Alabama, Colorado, Georgia, Illinois, Indiana, Iowa, Kentucky, Minnesota, Nebraska, Ohio, Oregon, South Dakota, Tennessee, Vermont, Washington, and Wisconsin.

ATHENS—The first American city to carry this name was founded in Georgia in 1801. It was selected after the Revolution during a period of classical naming. Athens, Greece, has always been associated with culture, learning, and education. Other places bearing the name of Athens are located in Alabama, Illinois, Indiana, Louisiana, Maine, Michigan, New York, Ohio, Tennessee, Texas, West Virginia, and Wisconsin.

ATLANTA—First used in Georgia in 1845, Atlanta is derived from a classical name and can also be found in Idaho, Illinois, Indiana, Kansas, Louisiana, Michigan, Missouri, Nebraska, New York, Ohio, and Texas. (See Chapter 8.)

AUBURN—Goldsmith's *The Deserted Village* was popular reading in the early nineteenth century, especially the line, "Sweet Auburn! loveliest village of the plain." Auburn was adopted as the corporate name for a town in Maine in 1805. Subsequently it has appeared in Alabama, California, Georgia, Illinois, Indiana, Iowa, Kansas, Kentucky, Massachusetts, Michigan, Nebraska, New

Hampshire, New York, Pennsylvania, Washington, West Virginia, and Wyoming.

AUGUSTA—Because Augusta was the daughter-in-law of King George II and Princess of Wales, townspeople in Georgia and Virginia selected the name. In Maine, however, the name was accepted in 1797 in honor of Pamela Augusta Dearborn, daughter of General Henry Dearborn. Augusta is repeated in Arkansas, Illinois, Kansas, Kentucky, Michigan, Missouri, Montana, New Jersey, Ohio, West Virginia, and Wisconsin.

AURORA—In New York State, the name is reputed to have been derived from an Iroquois word that meant "constant dawn." Interestingly enough, the word *aurora* is Latin for "dawn." In Ohio, the town Aurora was named for a woman. Whatever the derivation, there are cities and towns with this name in Arkansas, Colorado, Indiana, Iowa, Kansas, Maine, Missouri, Nebraska, North Carolina, Oregon, South Dakota, Utah, and West Virginia.

AUSTIN—In Texas, the city was named for Stephen F. Austin; in Minnesota, for Austin R. Nicholls, a first settler; and in Nevada, for George Austin, a town founder. It is repeated in Arkansas, Colorado, Indiana, Kentucky, Montana, and Pennsylvania.

AVALON—King Arthur and the knights of his Round Table thought of Avalon as a bit of paradise. After Tennyson's version of the King Arthur tales, *Idylls of the King,* had become popular, a Pennsylvania community adopted the name in 1893. It appeared previously as Lord Baltimore's abortive colony in Newfoundland and later in California, Mississippi, Missouri, New Jersey, Texas, and Wisconsin.

AVON—Following the Revolution, Americans began to read more and more, and they used their favorite phrases from literature in the naming of their homes. Shakespeare was a most popular author. And his title of "Bard of the Avon," a river in England, is commemorated in Colorado, Connecticut, Illinois, Massachusetts, Minnesota, Mississippi, Montana, New York, North Carolina, Ohio, and South Dakota.

BELLEVILLE—French for "beautiful village" or town, the phrase became popular with settlers who liked what they saw in

Arkansas, Illinois, Kansas, Michigan, New York, Pennsylvania, West Virginia, and Wisconsin.

BELLEVUE—Because the French helped the colonists to overthrow the domination of the English crown, the Americans used French phrases, such as *belle vue,* "beautiful view," to describe their settlements in Colorado, Idaho, Iowa, Maryland, Michigan, Nebraska, Ohio, Tennessee, Texas, and Washington.

BETHLEHEM—The Christian spirit filled many early Americans and they tried to impart this feeling to others. The name Bethlehem first appeared in Connecticut in 1739. On Christmas Eve two years later, Moravian settlers in Pennsylvania decided to name their new town Bethlehem. Bethlehems appear also in Georgia, Indiana, Kentucky, Maryland, and New Hampshire.

BRISTOL—After London, Bristol was the most important city in England. It first appeared as a name for American towns in Massachusetts, Pennsylvania, and Rhode Island. Towns in Colorado, Connecticut, Florida, Georgia, Illinois, Indiana, New Hampshire, South Dakota, Tennessee, Vermont, Virginia, West Virginia, and Wisconsin also carry the name.

BROOKLYN—Originally a part of the Dutch settlement of New Amsterdam (see Chapter 8), the name of Brooklyn has been carried to Alabama, Connecticut, Georgia, Illinois, Iowa, Kentucky, Michigan, Mississippi, Pennsylvania, Washington, West Virginia, and Wisconsin.

BURLINGTON—The New Jersey town that bears the name of Burlington was settled in the seventeenth century by immigrants from Bridlington, Yorkshire, England. At first the name was mispronounced, then misspelled into its current form. In 1763, a town was founded in Vermont, bearing the same name. It, however, was named for a prominent local family: the Burlings. Burlingtons appear in Colorado, Illinois, Indiana, Iowa, Kansas, Kentucky, Maine, Michigan, North Carolina, North Dakota, Oklahoma, Pennsylvania, Texas, Utah, Washington, West Virginia, Wisconsin, and Wyoming.

CAMBRIDGE—Some people in Maine in 1636 applied the name of a town and county in England to their own town and county with the idea of establishing a college there. The name migrated to Idaho, Illinois, Iowa, Kansas, Maryland, Massachusetts, Minnesota, Nebraska, New York, Ohio, Vermont, and Wisconsin.

CAMDEN—Charles Pratt, Lord Camden, was an early supporter of the American cause. His name is remembered in Alabama, Arkansas, Illinois, Indiana, Maine, Michigan, Mississippi, Missouri, New Jersey, New York, North Carolina, Ohio, South Carolina, Tennessee, Texas, and West Virginia.

CARLISLE—The name of an English city, Carlisle became the name of a Pennsylvania town in 1751. It is repeated in Arkansas, Indiana, Iowa, Kentucky, Louisiana, Massachusetts, Mississippi, New York, South Carolina, and West Virginia. Derived from the personal name, it appears elsewhere as Carlyle.

CLEVELAND—Though the Ohio city was named for General Moses Cleaveland (see Chapter 8), those in Iowa and Utah commemorate Grover Cleveland, President of the United States. Clevelands can be found on the map in Alabama, Arkansas, Georgia, Minnesota, Mississippi, Missouri, New Mexico, New York, North Carolina, North Dakota, Oklahoma, South Carolina, Tennessee, Texas, West Virginia, and Wisconsin.

COLUMBIA—After the Revolution, certain people were not too happy with their country's new name—The United States of America—and wanted something more descriptive. One suggestion, presented by Philip Freneau in his poem "American Liberty," was Columbia, in honor of Columbus, a name adopted by South Carolina in 1786 for the capital city. Columbia as a name still maintains some popularity. It appears in Alabama, California, Connecticut, Illinois, Iowa, Kentucky, Louisiana, Mississippi, Missouri, New Jersey, North Carolina, Pennsylvania, South Dakota, Tennessee, Utah, and Virginia.

DALLAS—Dallas, Pennsylvania, was named for the only Philadelphian who ever served as Vice-President, George Mifflin Dallas. He is also remembered in Georgia, Iowa, North Carolina, Oregon, South Dakota, Texas, West Virginia, and Wisconsin.

DAYTON—This city was founded by Jonathan Dayton in Ohio. The name also appears in Alabama, Idaho, Indiana, Iowa, Maryland, Michigan, Minnesota, Montana, Nevada, New Jersey, New

York, Oregon, Pennsylvania, Tennessee, Texas, Virginia, Washington, and Wyoming.

DECATUR—After the death of Commodore Stephen Decatur in 1820, President James Monroe, insisting that Decatur be commemorated, named a town in Alabama for him. The naval hero is further remembered in Arkansas, Illinois, Indiana, Iowa, Michigan, Nebraska, Ohio, Tennessee, Texas, and Washington.

DELAWARE—The states of Arkansas, Iowa, Kentucky, New Jersey, North Carolina, Ohio, and Oklahoma borrowed the name from either the state or the river.

DENVER—As a place name, Denver first appeared in Colorado in 1860 (see Chapter 8). It reappears in Arkansas, Illinois, Indiana, Iowa, Kentucky, Missouri, New York, Pennsylvania, and Tennessee.

DETROIT—Adapted from the French word *Ville d'étroit* (City of the strait), Detroit became the name of a city in Michigan. Other states to follow in using that name include Alabama, Illinois, Maine, Oregon, and Texas.

DOUGLAS—In Georgia and South Dakota, the people honored Stephen A. Douglas (1813–1861); in Arizona, they remembered Dr. J. S. Douglas, a town founder. The name is popular in Alabama, Alaska, Michigan, Nebraska, North Dakota, Oklahoma, Washington, and Wyoming.

DOVER—Delaware named its city for the English Channel port. In the Midwest and the South, the name was derived from the religious group the Dover Associates Report, which was well known in 1832. There are Dovers in Arkansas, Florida, Georgia, Idaho, Illinois, Kansas, Kentucky, Massachusetts, Minnesota, Missouri, New Hampshire, New Jersey, North Carolina, Oklahoma, Pennsylvania, and Tennessee.

EDEN—Eden is remembered from the Biblical story of Adam and Eve in the garden of paradise. Many Christian-oriented communities adopted the name. Eden, Texas, however, was named for Fred Eden, the first storekeeper. There are Edens in Arizona, Georgia, Idaho, Illinois, Maryland, Michigan, New York, South Dakota, Utah, Vermont, Wisconsin, and Wyoming.

EL DORADO—That legendary place (see Chapter 8) is used to

name towns or cities in Arkansas, California, Illinois, Kansas, Ohio, Oklahoma, Texas, and Wisconsin.

ELIZABETH—Obviously named for a woman, Elizabeth City, Virginia, founded in 1619, was named for Queen Elizabeth I; Cape Elizabeth, Maine, for the daughter of King James I; and in 1665, Elizabeth, New Jersey, for Elizabeth Carteret. Elizabeths are located in Arkansas, Colorado, Illinois, Indiana, Louisiana, Minnesota, Mississippi, Pennsylvania, and West Virginia.

ELKTON—Appearing as a place name in Florida, Kentucky, Michigan, Minnesota, Ohio, Oregon, South Dakota, Tennessee, and Virginia, it was first used in Maryland. Elks were an unusual sight to the colonists and they wanted to do honor to the good meat they had obtained.

EL PASO—In 1598, Juan de Oñate described finding the Rio Grande River at El Paso del Norte, "the pass of the north." Besides Texas, Arkansas and Illinois have towns named El Paso.

ENGLEWOOD—Created by a New Jersey real estate developer in 1859, the name suggested a suburban development and has been used in Colorado, Florida, Kansas, Ohio, and Tennessee.

FALMOUTH—According to the tradition of the day, Maine residents named their town in 1658 after one in England. Other towns with the same name are found in Indiana, Kentucky, Massachusetts, Michigan, and Virginia. The Kentucky town was named for the Virginia site in 1799.

FAYETTE—The Marquis de Lafayette's popularity increased after the Revolution and intensified when he returned to this country in 1824. He is remembered in Alabama, Iowa, Maine, Michigan, Mississippi, Missouri, New York, Ohio, and Utah, and elsewhere, as both Lafayette and La Fayette.

FLORENCE—In many cases, the towns named Florence honor a woman. However, the Alabama town was named by an Italian surveyor for his hometown. The name appears in Arizona, Indiana, Kansas, Kentucky, Minnesota, Mississippi, Missouri, Montana, New Jersey, Oregon, South Carolina, South Dakota, Texas, Vermont, and Wisconsin.

FRANKLIN—Not all Franklins are named for Benjamin Franklin. Though most of his namesake towns remember him for his connection with the early postal system, the Texas town was named for W. G. Franklin, an early settler. Franklins are found in Alabama, Arkansas, Georgia, Idaho, Illinois, Indiana, Kansas, Kentucky, Louisiana, Maine, Massachusetts, Minnesota, Missouri, Nebraska, New Hampshire, New Jersey, New York, North Carolina, Ohio, Pennsylvania, Tennessee, Vermont, Virginia, and West Virginia.

FREDERICKSBURG—The Virginia town was named for the Prince of Wales, son of King George II and father of King George III. Other Fredericksburgs are in Indiana, Iowa, Ohio, and Pennsylvania. The one in Texas was named to commemorate Frederick the Great. It was founded by German settlers in 1846.

GEORGETOWN—Many Georges are commemorated by this name, such as the town in South Carolina named for King George II; in Delaware for the 1791 town founder George Mitchell; in Kentucky for George Washington; the 1716 Maine town, for King George I. Cape George, by the way, was named for George Vancouver, who explored the northwest coast of America in 1792.

Georgetowns exist in Arkansas, California, Colorado, Connecticut, Florida, Georgia, Idaho, Illinois, Indiana, Louisiana, Maryland, Minnesota, Mississippi, New York, Ohio, Pennsylvania, Tennessee, and Texas.

GRANT—In most cases, especially in the West, this town name honors President Ulysses S. Grant. The name is also used in Alabama, Colorado, Florida, Iowa, Kentucky, Louisiana, Michigan, Montana, Nebraska, Oklahoma, and Virginia.

GREENVILLE—Sometimes, the name is used as a descriptive title, "the greeness of a town"; in other instances, for Revolutionary War General Nathanael Greene (1742–1786). There are Greenvilles in Alabama, California, Florida, Georgia, Illinois, Indiana, Iowa, Kentucky, Maine, Michigan, Mississippi, Missouri, New Hampshire, New York, North Carolina, Ohio, Pennsylvania, Rhode Island, South Carolina, Utah, Virginia, West Virginia, and Wisconsin.

HALIFAX—The town of Halifax, Massachusetts, settled in 1734, was named for an English town. Six years later some people in New Hampshire gave the same name to one of their towns, but in this case, they named it for the second Earl of Halifax, who was quite active in colonial affairs.

The name also appears in North Carolina, Pennsylvania, and Virginia.

HANOVER—Towns of this name were named after the city in Germany and the House of Hanover, which was the ruling house of the English monarchy from 1714 to 1775. The first town to bear this name was founded in 1727 in Massachusetts.

Hanovers appear in Arkansas, Connecticut, Illinois, Indiana, Kansas, Maine, Maryland, Michigan, Minnesota, New Hampshire, New Jersey, New Mexico, Pennsylvania, Virginia, West Virginia, and Wisconsin.

HARLEM—The name was first used in New York when that city was under Dutch control, after the city of the same name in the Netherlands. It appears in the United States in Georgia and Montana.

HARRISBURG—The first Harrisburg was the Pennsylvania town —now the capital—laid out by John Harris, Jr., in 1785.

There are Harrisburgs in Illinois, Missouri, Nebraska, North Carolina, Ohio, Oregon, and South Dakota.

HAVANA—There are Havanas, named for the Cuban city, in Alabama, Arkansas, Florida, Illinois, Kansas, and North Dakota.

HUNTSVILLE—Huntsville, Alabama, was settled by John Hunt, who donated his name. Huntsville, Texas, was founded by an emigrant from Alabama. There are Huntsvilles in Arkansas, Illinois, Kentucky, Missouri, Ohio, Tennessee, Utah, and Washington.

INDEPENDENCE—Most Independences—found in California, Iowa, Kansas, Kentucky, Louisiana, Mississippi, Missouri, Oregon, Pennsylvania, Virginia, West Virginia, and Wisconsin—were named in a spirit of patriotism or were settled on the Fourth of July. Independence, Texas, on the other hand, founded in 1836, was given the name in commemoration of that territory's independence from Mexico.

JACKSON—Most of the towns with this name honor Andrew Jackson, President of the United States. They appear in Alabama, Georgia, Kentucky, Louisiana, Michigan, Minnesota, Mississippi,

Missouri, Montana, Nebraska, New Hampshire, New Jersey, North Carolina, Ohio, Pennsylvania, South Carolina, Tennessee, Wisconsin, and Wyoming. Jackson Hole, Wyoming, is an exception. It was named for D. E. Jackson, an early fur trader.

JAMESTOWN—On the coast of Virginia is the most noted of all the Jamestowns, so named on May 14, 1607, "in honor of the King's [James I] most excellent majesty." The others that followed are situated in Alabama, Arkansas, California, Colorado, Indiana, Kansas, Kentucky, Louisiana, Maryland, Michigan, New York, North Carolina, North Dakota, Ohio, Pennsylvania, Rhode Island, South Carolina, and Tennessee.

JEFFERSON—Thomas Jefferson, author and signer of the Declaration of Independence among other things, wrote: "Death alone can seal the title of any man to this honor [having something named after him], by putting it out of his power to forfeit it." He was honored in Alabama, Arkansas, Colorado, Georgia, Iowa, Maine, Maryland, Massachusetts, New Hampshire, New York, North Carolina, Ohio, Oklahoma, Oregon, Pennsylvania, South Carolina, South Dakota, Texas, Virginia, and Wisconsin.

KENSINGTON—The name of a village in England, now a part of London, lives on in Connecticut, Georgia, Kansas, Maryland, Minnesota, and Ohio.

KENT—The original settlements in Delaware, 1683, and Connecticut, 1738, were named for the English county. In Ohio, Kent was named in 1864 for a local businessman's family, while in Oregon the name was drawn from a hat and selected because it was "nice and short." Kents appear also in Alabama, Illinois, Iowa, Minnesota, New York, Pennsylvania, and Washington.

KNOX—General Henry Knox (1750–1806) of Revolutionary War fame is remembered in towns of this name in Indiana, New York, North Dakota, and Pennsylvania. He is further recalled in towns with the name Knoxville.

LANCASTER—Named after the English town and county, Lancaster first appeared as a Virginia county in 1651; two years later, it became the name of a town in Massachusetts.

Other Lancasters are in California, Illinois, Kansas, Kentucky,

Minnesota, Missouri, New Hampshire, New York, Ohio, Pennsylvania, South Carolina, Tennessee, Texas, Virginia, Washington, and Wisconsin.

LA SALLE—Robert Cavelier, Sieur de La Salle (1643–1687), was a noted French explorer. His name is carried on in Colorado, Illinois, Michigan, Minnesota, and Texas. He was too famous, in some respects. When Philadelphia sportswriters were trying to supply a nickname for the LaSalle College basketball team, they decided on "The Explorers"—forgetting that the founder of the Christian Brothers religious order was another La Salle, no relation to the explorer.

LEXINGTON—The town of Lexington, Massachusetts, was named in 1713 for a village in England, now spelled Laxton. Following the "shot heard 'round the world," very few namers thought of Lexington in the English context again. The sacrifice of the men at Lexington is remembered in Alabama, Georgia, Illinois, Indiana, Kentucky, Michigan, Mississippi, Missouri, Nebraska, New York, North Carolina, Oklahoma, South Carolina, Tennessee, Texas, and Virginia.

LINCOLN—Though most of our contemporaries can only think of any place named Lincoln as commemorating Abraham Lincoln, it was used first in Maine as a county and in Massachusetts as a town, long before the Revolution, after the town and county in England. After the war, counties in Georgia and North Carolina adopted the name to honor General Benjamin Lincoln. Lincoln, Nebraska, honors the fallen President, while the California town carries the middle name of its founder.

Lincolns exist in Alabama, Arkansas, Delaware, Illinois, Iowa, Kansas, Kentucky, Maine, Michigan, Missouri, Montana, New Hampshire, New Mexico, Pennsylvania, Texas, Vermont, Virginia, and Washington.

MANCHESTER—Manchester, Massachusetts, was named after the English city. When the Duke of Manchester visited New Hampshire, another town was so named.

There are Manchesters in California, Connecticut, Georgia, Illinois, Iowa, Kansas, Kentucky, Maine, Maryland, Michigan, Minnesota, New York, Oklahoma, Pennsylvania, Texas, Utah, Washington, and Wisconsin.

MANTUA—Mantua, Italy, was the home of the poet Virgil. The name was used in Alabama during the classical resurgence following the Revolution. In Ohio, the name was given to a town after news reached that area that Napoleon had scored a victory at Mantua in 1796.

MONMOUTH—Monmouth is another transplanted English place name. It was used in New Jersey and was the place where George Washington decided to take on the British following their withdrawal from Philadelphia in 1778. Unfortunately, Monmouth Court House, New Jersey, is now called Freehold.

Monmouth's tradition is carried on by the states of Illinois, Iowa, Maine, and Oregon.

MONTGOMERY—Most namers contend that the proliferation of Montgomerys in the United States is there to honor General Richard Montgomery, a Revolutionary War officer. In Alabama, Montgomery County was named in 1816 for Major L. P. Montgomery, who had been killed in the Creek war. The city to bear that name was announced in 1819—in honor of General Richard Montgomery, officially. When Montgomery County, Pennsylvania, was carved out of Philadelphia, the two government officials who pushed the name were both Montgomerys.

There is a Montgomery in each of the following states: Alabama, Illinois, Indiana, Iowa, Louisiana, Michigan, Minnesota, New York, Pennsylvania, Texas, Vermont, and West Virginia.

MONTICELLO—The Italian word for "little mountain" was made famous by Thomas Jefferson when he selected it for his beautiful home in Virginia. Because of his use, and the term's suggestion of height, the name Monticello appears in Arkansas, Florida, Georgia, Illinois, Indiana, Iowa, Kentucky, Maine, Minnesota, Mississippi, Missouri, New Mexico, New York, South Carolina, Utah, and Wisconsin.

MOUNT VERNON—Mount Vernon was Lawrence Washington's home. The name became quite popular after his brother George moved in. It is repeated in Alabama, Arkansas, Illinois, Indiana, Iowa, Kentucky, Maine, Missouri, New Hampshire, New York, Ohio, Oregon, South Dakota, Tennessee, and Washington.

NAPOLEON—Several of these towns were named for the "Little Corporal," such as Napoleon, Ohio, which was settled by the French. In North Dakota, however, the name came from Napoleon Goodsill, president of the townsite company.

There are Napoleons in Indiana, Michigan, and Missouri.

NAZARETH—As with Bethlehem, this name was used for its Biblical meaning. In most cases, such as the 1741 Pennsylvania town of Bethlehem founded by Count Zinzendorf and his Moravians, towns with Biblical names were settled by Protestant sects. In Texas, however, Nazareth received its name from a Roman Catholic priest. Nazareths can also be found in Kentucky and Michigan.

NEWARK—The first Newark was founded in 1666 in New Jersey. Some people suggest that the name had religious connotations, such as "new ark." But the town was settled by people from Connecticut who were imbued with the concept of naming their towns after places in England. There is a Newark in England.

Newark appears also as a town name in California, Delaware, Illinois, Maryland, New York, and Ohio.

NEW CASTLE—In 1664, Colonel Richard Nicolls named the former Swedish/Dutch settlement in Delaware for the Earl of New Castle. In 1802, Pennsylvania named a town New Castle, after the English city.

Alabama, California, Colorado, Indiana, Kentucky, Maine, Nebraska, New Hampshire, Oklahoma, Texas, Utah, Virginia, and Wyoming are states that have either a New Castle or a Newcastle in them.

NEWFOUNDLAND—Though there is a land called Newfoundland, most uses of the name do not commemorate that island. Instead, newly discovered land was given the name for its literal meaning. The name appears in Kentucky, New Jersey, and Pennsylvania.

ONEIDA—Oneida was the name of an Indian tribe and has been used for town and city names in Arkansas, Illinois, Kansas, Kentucky, New York, Pennsylvania, Tennessee, and Wisconsin.

ORANGE—Though most people contend that the town name is derived from the Prince of Orange, a Dutch title, the Indian tribal name for the New Jersey area, settled in 1655, was Auronge. In other places, such as California, the name was obtained from the citrus fruit exported from that state.

Other towns named Orange can be found in Connecticut, Massachusetts, and Virginia.

OXFORD—Oxford is a town and a university in England. Its name was taken in Maryland, 1683, and in Massachusetts, 1693. Its use was continued in Florida, Georgia, Indiana, Iowa, Kansas, Louisiana, Maine, Michigan, Mississippi, Nebraska, New Jersey, New York, North Carolina, Ohio, Pennsylvania, and Wisconsin.

PAOLI—Paoli began in Pennsylvania as a tavern that bore the name of Pasquale Paoli, leader of a Corsican revolt in the middle of the eighteenth century. The town name can also be found in Colorado, Indiana, and Oklahoma.

PHILADELPHIA—The "City of Brotherly Love" (see Chapter 3) appears in Mississippi, Missouri, New York, and Tennessee. In Ohio, there is a city named New Philadelphia.

PLYMOUTH—John Smith's 1616 map erased Indian names and replaced them with transplants from England. The name of the 1620 Pilgrim settlement in Massachusetts could have been derived from Smith's map, but the group that settled there had been chartered by the Plymouth Company and had sailed from the port of Plymouth in Devonshire, England.

There are Plymouths in California, Connecticut, Florida, Illinois, Indiana, Iowa, Maine, Michigan, Nebraska, New Hampshire, New York, North Carolina, Ohio, Pennsylvania, Vermont, Washington, and Wisconsin.

PORTLAND—Though the town in Maine had other names, it became Portland in 1786, because that was what it was: "port land." Oregon borrowed the name in 1845 when town namers flipped a coin to choose either Portland or Boston as a name for their new town. Other states, which did not flip a coin but selected the name of Portland, include Arkansas, Connecticut, Michigan, Missouri, North Dakota, Ohio, Pennsylvania, and Tennessee. Portland, Indiana, was named for the cement; Portland, Texas, because it was "port land."

QUINCY—The first Quincy, which is in Massachusetts, was named in 1792 for Colonel John Quincy. Illinois, at a later date, named its Quincy for John Quincy Adams, President of the United States. It was necessary to use his middle name because his father, the second President, had been honored with the use of his last name.

There are Quincys in California, Florida, Indiana, Kansas, Kentucky, Michigan, Missouri, Ohio, Pennsylvania, and Washington.

RICHMOND—William Byrd named his town in Virginia in 1733 after Richmond in Surrey on the Thames because he thought the two sites had strong resemblances. In 1765, Massachusetts had its own Richmond, this one named for the Duke of Richmond, a sympathizer with the colonial cause.

Richmonds exist in California, Illinois, Indiana, Kansas, Kentucky, Maine, Michigan, Missouri, Ohio, Texas, Utah, and Vermont.

SPRINGFIELD—In 1641 the Massachusetts Springfield was named for the English village. The one in South Carolina grew out of the fields of a man named Spring. Usually, the term is descriptive—and not for an individual.

There are Springfields in Arkansas, Colorado, Georgia, Illinois, Kentucky, Louisiana, Maine, Minnesota, Missouri, Nebraska, New Jersey, Ohio, Oregon, South Dakota, Tennessee, Vermont, Virginia, and Wisconsin.

UTICA—During the period of classical naming, Erastus Clark, a lawyer, suggested this name for the 1798 New York town. Utica was an ancient city of Africa, so it is more likely that he was thinking about Cato Uticensis, the defender of Republican ideals who committed suicide after Julius Caesar's victory at the battle of Thapsus.

WASHINGTON—All of the cities, towns, and villages that bear this name have some relation to George Washington, "Father of His Country." His name appears in Arkansas, California, Connecticut, Georgia, Illinois, Indiana, Iowa, Kansas, Kentucky, Louisiana, Maine, Michigan, Mississippi, Missouri, Nebraska, New Hampshire, New Jersey, North Carolina, Oklahoma, Pennsylvania, Utah, Vermont, Virginia, Washington, West Virginia, and in the District of Columbia. By act of Congress in 1853, the State of Washington was named after the first President.

WATERLOO—Waterloo was a small, unknown village in Belgium until Napoleon was defeated there in 1815. The battle received a great deal of publicity in this country and it came to mean "a defeat." An anti-Napoleonist gave the name to his New York town; in Oregon, the name was used after a severe court decision was rendered.

Waterloos exist in Alabama, Arkansas, Illinois, Indiana, Iowa, Montana, Nebraska, Ohio, South Carolina, and Wisconsin.

WINONA—Winona, a Sioux name, was usually given to the firstborn daughter. It appeared as a town name in 1853, in Minnesota. The town by that name in Texas honored Winona Douglas, the daughter of a local railroad owner.

Other Winonas include cities and towns in Michigan, Mississippi, Missouri, Ohio, Tennessee, Washington, and West Virginia.

YOUNGSTOWN—The 1797 Ohio settlement was named for John Young, who helped found the town. Youngstowns also appear in Florida, New York, and Pennsylvania.

There are many, many more transported and transplanted names in the United States. In some respects, it took less imagination to adopt a name than to create a brand-new one. But do not be dismayed, the American mind created a vast number of unique, sometimes puzzling place names.

You might note that a particular duplicated name is not listed in your state. We have listed only those cities which have their own post offices and zip codes. There are, however, cities and towns that do in fact exist, but not in the eyes of the Postal Service. Their naming may be just as intriguing as the stories told above.

Three Log Houses

When an explorer first sighted land, a body of water, a mountain, or a potential townsite, he immediately planted his flag and proceeded to name the place.

Depending on his personal and political leanings and his desire for fame and fortune, he might decide on a title that would enhance his position and help advance his ends. If he did not feel that naming the place after his "protector" or a patron saint would help him in this world or the next, he might simply decide to commemorate himself or a member of his own family.

Since there were no rules or regulations to govern his choice, he was free to do whatever he wished. As the period of global exploration came to a close and the effort for national discovery and settlement began, ordinary citizens got into the act and named anything that didn't already have a name—and renamed many that did.

With an abundance of land, speculators affixed names to towns and cities before the first spade of dirt was turned. Philadelphia, Pennsylvania, as one example, was named before William Penn even saw it. He had plans drawn up and then attempted to sell to the British or Europeans his American city lots, and, as an inducement, country estates as a bonus. William Penn was not unique—he was only one of the first.

Others, drawn by the lure of high profits for small investment, did much the same thing.

It was far less expensive, they learned, to hire an engineer or an architect to draw up grandiose plans than actually to construct a town. These ploys prompted Horace Greeley to say, "It takes three log houses to make a city in Kansas, but they begin calling it a city so soon as they have staked out the lots."

If, as Greeley implied, a city was more than "three log houses," what then was it?

A city is usually a large or important town, incorporated and governed by a mayor and a body of councilmen or aldermen. A town, on the other hand, is a thickly populated area, smaller than a city, but larger than a village. Like a city, it too has fixed boundaries and certain local powers of self-government. For the sake of convenience, one can say that a town is any urban area, as contrasted with the surrounding countryside.

A village is a small community, or a group of houses in a rural area. It is larger than a hamlet and usually smaller than a town. A hamlet, the smallest community, is nothing more than a small village. In fact, in England a hamlet is a village without benefit of a church of its own.

For the settling and pioneering thousands, what was built was not necessarily what was dreamed. A hamlet, tucked away in the woods, might, they felt, grow by leaps and bounds into the great city of the future. No one knew for sure how much grit and determination would be poured into a little community, what industry might take a liking to the location, what affluent individuals would arrive and help them lift the tiny area into the stars.

So the pioneers named the little places with names that promised greatness. No one bothered to tell them their dreams might never reach reality. They were free to use whichever or whatever name they desired. No one sought to correct the name of a river that was called one thing on one side and something else on the other. And no one interfered with the naming of several cities or towns in the same state with identical names. Perhaps they were named before state boundaries were set. No one really cared, because names were important only to the people who used them.

Names were also important to later generations to give clues to what the land was like before development took over.

The following place names give some inkling of the way things were:

ARIZONA

TUCSON—Originally settled as an Indian village, Tucson was renamed Presidio de San Augustín de Tuguison by Spanish conquerors. The name was shortened to Tucson after the town was transferred to the United States as part of the Gadsden Purchase, 45,000 square miles bought from Mexico, now part of New Mexico and Arizona.

CALIFORNIA

CASTRO VALLEY—Long before Cuba had a leader by the same name, Castro Valley was settled on a section of a Mexican land grant that had been made to Don Guillermo Castro in 1841.

LOS ANGELES—This western metropolis was originally a cattle-farming center with the unwieldy name of El Pueblo de Nuestra Señora la Reina de los Angeles de la Porciuncula in 1781. "Our Lady" has been forgotten, but not her charges, the angels.

OAKLAND—During the Mexican days of California, there was a small town known as Encinal del Temescal, the "oak-grove of the sweat-house." The American settlers weren't too well versed in Spanish, but they could see the trees and they called their community Oakland.

VALLEJO—This town was founded by Admiral David Farragut around 1850 on the land of General Mariano G. Vallejo.

VENTURA—That is not the official corporate name of this city. Founded in 1782, it was the site of San Buenaventura Mission. The correct name is Buenaventura.

COLORADO

DENVER—Denver was created in 1860 by the incorporation of three villages. It was named in honor of the territorial governor of Kansas, James W. Denver. The territory of Kansas, at the time, also included the eastern sections of the present State of Colorado.

CONNECTICUT

BRANFORD—When it was settled in 1644, it was known as Wethersfield. Later the name was changed to commemorate Brentford, England, with a slightly altered spelling.

GEORGIA

ATLANTA—The Creek Indians ceded the land for this city to the State of Georgia in 1821. It was settled in 1833. Four years later it was founded as a town, located at the end of the Western & Atlantic Railroad, and called Terminus. Terminus was incorporated as Marthasville in 1834. In 1845, railroad builder J. E. Thompson renamed it Atlanta.

HAWAII

CAPTAIN COOK—The name of a town on the island of Hawaii. The name commemorates the great British seafaring explorer who was killed and buried in Hawaii.

HILO—A city on the island of Hawaii. An ancient Polynesian navigator is honored here.

HONOLULU—The name of a city on Oahu. In Polynesian it means "calm bay" or "protected harbor."

LIHUE—This town was so named because of the constant "cool breeze." It is on the island of Kauai.

OAHU—On this island, known as the "gathering place," native kings met and tribal leaders gathered.

WAILUKU—The name of a city on the island of Maui. The word means "breaking waves."

ILLINOIS

CAHOKIA—The first permanent settlement in Illinois was established here in 1699 as a French mission. It derived its name from the Cahokie Indians, who once inhabited the area.

GALESBURG—Founded by a group of pioneers from the Mohawk Valley, Galesburg was not named for any gust of wind. It was named for the leader of the expedition, George Washington Gale.

JOLIET—Though Louis Joliet, a French explorer, first visited the area with Jacques Marquette in 1673, the city to bear his name was not settled until 1831.

INDIANA

HAMMOND—When the town was settled in 1851, the townspeople honored George Hammond, founder of the meat-packing plant and the major local employer.

TWIN FALLS—This city is located on the Snake River and named for the falls that divide into two channels, drop two hundred feet, and then reunite.

IOWA

BETTENDORF—Though colonized in 1840, the city was re-named for W. P. Bettendorf in 1903. He established a railroad equipment business in the town a year earlier.

DUBUQUE—Named in 1788 for lead miner Julien Dubuque, the city was not settled permanently until 1833.

MASON CITY—Members of the Order of Masons founded this town in 1853.

KENTUCKY

COVINGTON—Incorporated in 1834, the city was named for General Leonard Covington, a hero in the War of 1812.

MARYLAND

ANNAPOLIS—It was founded in 1649 by settlers seeking religious freedom and was called Providence. In 1695, the name was changed to Annapolis, and then chartered by Queen Anne in 1708.

BETHESDA—Settled in the late seventeenth century by Scottish, English, and Irish colonists, the city obtained its name from the Bethesda Presbyterian Church, built there in 1820.

CHEVY CHASE—This suburban Washington, D.C., community, incorporated in 1914, was developed on and around the estate of Joseph Belt (1690–1761). Belt's estate was known as Cheivy Chace. The highway that bypasses the nation's capital, however, is not named after Mr. Belt.

MASSACHUSETTS

AMHERST—Incorporated in 1759, this college town was named in honor of the general in charge of the British forces in America during the French and Indian War—Baron Jeffrey Amherst.

BOSTON—John Winthrop and his band of Puritans founded the

city in 1630 and named it after a town in Lincolnshire, England.

HOLYOKE—This town derives its name from a pioneer settler, Elizur Holyoke.

MICHIGAN

CADILLAC—Not to be confused with the automobile of the same name, this city, located on the Cadillac and Mitchell Lakes, was named for Sieur Antoine de la Mothe Cadillac, the explorer who founded Detroit. Cadillac was settled in 1871.

HOLLAND—One would imagine that this town was founded by Dutch settlers. It was—in 1847. Even today, Holland remembers its heritage with an annual tulip festival.

WYANDOTTE—Founded in 1818, this city is situated on the former site of a village of the Wyandotte Indians.

MINNESOTA

BLAINE—First organized as a township in 1877, the city was named for Senator James Gillespie Blaine. He ran as a Republican for the Presidency in 1884, and lost to Grover Cleveland.

DULUTH—Sieur Daniel Greysolon Duluth first visited this area in 1679. Nothing much happened there until 1792, when a trading post was established on the site. The city was founded in 1856.

MINNEAPOLIS—When the white men came to this section of the territory, they were impressed with the beauty of a waterfall. Thinking themselves smart, they named the falls Minnehaha from their own understanding of the Indian language. Unfortunately, they were redundant in their choice of words, because *minne* means water and *haha* means waterfalls. In other words, they named it "Water waterfalls Falls." This redundancy didn't stop with them. The founders of this city took the name of the falls, added to it the Greek word for city, *polis,* and came up with Minneapolis.

MONTANA

BOZEMAN—Named for explorer John M. Bozeman, this city was founded in 1864. Bozeman blazed a trail, which also bears his name, through the wilderness. After 1877, the Bozeman Trail became an important cattle route.

NEVADA

CARSON CITY—Eagle Station was what they called it in 1851. Later it was renamed for Christopher "Kit" Carson, legendary trapper, guide, and Civil War general. Carson City was incorporated in 1875.

NEW JERSEY

IRVINGTON—The original settlement of 1692 was known as Camptown. It was renamed in 1852 for author Washington Irving, who wrote the story of the Headless Horseman.

NEW MEXICO

ALBUQUERQUE—The Spanish founded this place in 1706. It was used as a military post until 1870. Ten years later, a new city was founded and named for Affonso de Albuquerque, a Portuguese admiral who founded his nation's empire in the Orient.

NEW YORK

THE BRONX—This borough of New York City was founded in 1641 by Jonas Bronck for the Dutch West India Company. It became part of the largest city in the United States in 1898.

BROOKLYN—Another well-known New York borough, it was founded by Dutch and Walloons in 1636–1637. The first settlement in 1645 was named Breuckelen. Thinking it too Dutch-sounding, English settlers later Anglicized the name.

COOPERSTOWN—The home of the Baseball Hall of Fame was founded by William Cooper in 1785. He was the father of James Fenimore Cooper, author of romantic tales of frontier life.

MANHATTAN—In 1626, Peter Minuit purchased the entire island from the Manhattan Indians.

WEST POINT—The scene of Benedict Arnold's treason and home of the U.S. Military Academy, West Point, was named because of its location—the west bank of the Hudson River.

OHIO

CINCINNATI—Originally a fort established by the United States in 1789 to quell Indian disturbances, it was called Losantiville. In 1790, the name was changed to commemorate the Revolutionary War Society of the Cincinnati. The Society, formed by members of General Washington's officer cadre, thought of the general as the embodiment of the Roman hero Cincinnatus.

CLEVELAND—Long before Grover Cleveland was born, Cleveland existed. It was founded in 1796 by Moses Cleaveland, and chartered in 1836. The "a" was eliminated by a local newspaper because Cleaveland's name was one letter too wide for the masthead.

FAIRBORN—Two small communities—Fairfield, founded in 1799, and Osborn, 1853—were merged into one in 1950. To placate both groups of citizens, the combined name was presented and accepted as the new town's name.

TOLEDO—Formed from the union of Port Lawrence and Vistula in 1833, Toledo was named for the Spanish city, one of that country's most historical and architecturally important sites. After a border dispute with Michigan, Toledo became part of Ohio in 1835.

YOUNGSTOWN—In 1797, John Young bought the area upon which this city now stands from the Western Reserve Land Company. It was incorporated in 1848.

ZANESVILLE—When Ebenezer Zane founded it in 1797, the area was nothing but wilderness. Half a century later, Zanesville was a city.

OREGON

ASTORIA—This was the first permanent U.S. settlement on the West Coast. It was founded in 1811 by John Jacob Astor's Pacific Fur Company.

PENNSYLVANIA

ERIE—This city, laid out in 1795, was named for the Indian tribe, which was also known as the Cat Nation.

WILKES-BARRE—Settled in 1769, the town was named for John

Wilkes and Isaac Barre, supporters of the colonial cause in Parliament during the days that preceded the American Revolution.

RHODE ISLAND

WARWICK—Originally called Shawomet, for the Indian tribe from whom the land was purchased, it was founded by Samuel Gorton and incorporated in 1644. The town was later renamed in honor of the Lord of Warwick.

TEXAS

ABILENE—Herds of cattle were driven from this area to Abilene, Kansas. When settled as a railway junction, the Texas town assumed the name of the city from which it received its wealth.

ALICE—Settled in 1886, the town was named for Alice Kleberg, a local rancher.

AUSTIN—When settlers founded this place in 1835, they called it Waterloo. Incorporated as a city in 1839, it was renamed for Stephen F. Austin.

BEAUMONT—The first settlers to this spot were French and Spanish fur trappers and explorers. Apparently the French influence was dominant. The name given to the town in 1825 is of French origin and means "beautiful mountain."

BROWNSVILLE—General Zachary Taylor established a military post here in 1846 and named it Fort Brown, for Major Jacob Brown.

CORPUS CHRISTI—Alonso de Pineda, a Spanish explorer, spied this site in the sixteenth century. The particular day was Corpus Christi Day. The city was incorporated in 1852. The name translates as "body of Christ."

DENTON—John B. Denton was a lawyer and minister who had been killed by Indians. When the town was founded in 1855, it was named in his memory.

HOUSTON—This city was founded in 1836 and named for Sam Houston, the first president of Texas. That same year was the first year of the Republic of Texas.

KINGSVILLE—Kingsville has no relationship whatsoever to the monarch of any foreign country. Settled in 1902, it is the headquarters of the nearly two-thousand-square-mile King Ranch, founded in 1853 by Richard King.

WACO—This town was settled on the site of a former village of the Waco Indians in 1849.

VIRGINIA

CHARLOTTESVILLE—Founded in 1762, the city was named for Queen Charlotte of England.

FREDERICKSBURG—Home of George Washington's mother and the scene of one of the bloodiest battles of the Civil War, Fredericksburg was laid out in 1727 and named for King George III's father.

NEWPORT NEWS—Two Irishmen, named Newce, came to the Virginia shores and founded a new community. They differed from most newcomers because they already had experience— they had settled and founded Newce in Ireland.

Their Virginia colony carried the same name, prefixed by the words New Port, since the town was on the water and since it was brand-new.

As time went on, the Newce boys were forgotten, but the people recalled Captain Newport, who helped found Virginia. And Newce, to be sure, was harder to spell than News, so the Irishmen's settlement became known as Newport News.

WASHINGTON

BREMERTON—This place was named for William Bremer who founded the townsite and established the Puget Sound Naval Shipyard there in 1891.

SEATTLE—A young Indian, known for his strength and agility, matured into a vicious adult. "Chief See-yat," a trader wrote, "has murdered an Indian doctor. . . . I wish," he added, "they would determine on shooting the villain."

As he aged, See-yat mellowed and finally allowed a missionary to baptize him as Noah Sealth. By 1853, Noah, formerly See-yat, was a gregarious old man, loved and admired by the settlers. When they laid out their town in Washington State, they called it after him, Seattle.

VANCOUVER—Originally founded as a Hudson's Bay Company post in 1824, the town was named after Vancouver, British Columbia. (See Chapter 7.)

WISCONSIN
WEST ALLIS—Settled in 1827 as Honey Creek, the town changed its name in 1902 to reflect the area's biggest employer, the Allis-Chalmers Manufacturing Company.

Shortly before the end of the nineteenth century, certain government officials in Washington began to feel that the common people of America had had enough fun. It was time for order to be restored to the naming chaos.

In 1889, the government offices that were responsible for developing the maps and drawings that represented America, such as the Coast and Geodetic Survey, the Hydrographic Office, the Geological Survey, the Departments of State and War, all had different names for the same places. This would not do—not in the United States.

Besides, for each name they had, the Post Office Department had a different one. It was quite confusing.

On September 4, 1890, by Executive Order, President Benjamin Harrison established the Board on Geographic Names.

Within a year, the board, a group of ten practical men, had drawn up a set of standards for the naming of places in the United States.

The first principle of naming, as these men saw it, was "that spelling and pronunciation which is sanctioned by local usage should in general be adopted." If local custom was divided, preference, they conceded, should be given to that which was "most appropriate and euphonious."

Another principle, as laid down by the board, outlawed the use of "city" and "-town" as parts of a name, the "h" in "-burgh," and the "ugh" in "-borough."

No self-respecting American pioneer could accept sitting down something as un-American as that. There had always been fear of foreign domination of the American territory and the removal of "h" from *-burgh* smacked of an insidious German influence.

It was the individual citizen's constitutional right to fight to protect and preserve those names held dear. Pittsburgh was one city that proudly defended its right to retain the English spelling of its suffix.

The problems were not only created by inventive citizens. "To a much greater extent," the board reported, "than the railroads has the Post-Office Department confused the nomenclature of the smaller towns and villages by attaching names to the post-offices not in accordance with those in local usage."

That remark struck a blow against a venerable American institution. Postmasters had been allowed the privilege of naming their towns any way they saw fit. Many times they named the town after a most notable personage—themselves.

Regardless of the furor that such a statement must have stirred, the Post Office Department standardized the post offices, according to board regulations, in 1894.

Another principle: "In the case of names consisting of more than one word, it is desirable," the board declared, "to combine them into one word." That, they found, didn't always work. They had to relent in some areas before they created such monstrosities as Newyork, Birdinhand, Fortwashington, Marthasvineyard, and others.

Under the board's recommended principles, many towns capitulated, others did not. They had labored too long and hard to allow any bureaucrat the right to take from them the immortality of a name.

Perhaps the board realized that the American mind is quick, and devious. Perhaps they were frightened of the reputation a country would obtain from flamboyant, exotic, or "cute" names.

No board, no group of citizens, no one was going to tell ordinary, run-of-the-mill Americans that they couldn't call a town by the name of their choice.

Picking Up the Mail

When mail service began in the United States, it was not as we know it today. Mail was not delivered to each person's home. Rather, it was dispatched to a centralized location to which every citizen had access.

The most popular distribution centers for mail, news, and gossip were the taverns, inns, and stores that peppered the countryside. Early travelers would stop at a local tavern or inn for food, refreshment, and lodging—and the latest news.

Since the horsemen who first carried the mail—and later the coaches—needed to refresh their mounts, as well as themselves, the taverns and inns were also logical places to leave the mail.

When postal service became more organized, and authorities tried to attach names to the communities to which mail was sent, they decided, with the townspeople's agreement, to call the town by the same name as the mail drop. Later, the focal point of the community centered on the general store. The storekeeper became the postmaster, and the name of his store became the name of the town.

Because of this, many American towns and cities have strange and wonderful names.

ALABAMA: Owens Cross Roads
ARIZONA: Silver Bell
IDAHO: Macks Inn
KENTUCKY: Webbs Cross Roads
MARYLAND: Rising Sun

MICHIGAN: Rives Junction
NEW HAMPSHIRE: Willey House
NEW JERSEY: Whitehouse
NEW YORK: Barnes Corners, Clinton Corners, Hayt Corners, Kelly
   Corners, Oaks Corners, Paul Smiths, Porter Corners, Rock Tav-
   ern
OHIO: White Cottage, Whitehouse
OKLAHOMA: Big Cabin
PENNSYLVANIA: Bird In Hand, Blue Ball, Blue Bell, Columbia
   Cross Roads, Forbes Road, King of Prussia, Paoli, Yellow House
SOUTH CAROLINA: Cross Anchor, Fountain Inn, Moncks Corner
TENNESSEE: Cypress Inn, Five Points, Pressmen's Home, White
   House
TEXAS: Bee House, Chapman Ranch, Whitehouse
UTAH: Rubys Inn
VIRGINIA: Browns Store, James Store, Kents Store, Millers Tavern,
   Steeles Tavern, Woods Cross Roads
WEST VIRGINIA: Keslers Cross Lanes
WISCONSIN: Hales Corner

The more intriguing names, such as Cross Anchor, South Carolina; Bird In Hand, Blue Ball, Blue Bell, and King of Prussia, Pennsylvania; Rising Sun, Maryland; and Silver Bell, Arizona, were
derived from signboards that attracted patrons. Many of these
early advertising devices were intricate works of art, lost in antiq-
uity and currently replaced by neon and plastic.

Besides the taverns, inns, and stores, early Americans also found
it convenient to accept delivery of mail at river and lake crossings.
Since waterways were important to them, it was logical for the
latter-day post offices to bear appropriate names.

ALABAMA: Millers Ferry, Moores Bridge
ALASKA: Cooper Landing
CALIFORNIA: Fields Landing, Knights Landing
CONNECTICUT: Gales Ferry
IDAHO: Bonners Ferry, Glenns Ferry
INDIANA: Paris Crossing

KENTUCKY: Cloyds Landing, Old Landing
MARYLAND: Tracys Landing
MICHIGAN: Bruce Crossing
MINNESOTA: Reads Landing
MISSOURI: Portage Des Sioux
NEBRASKA: Beaver Crossing
NEW JERSEY: Hancocks Bridge, Mays Landing
NEW YORK: Bolton Landing, Chenango Bridge, Dobbs Ferry, Fishers Landing, Glenwood Landing, Goldens Bridge, Huletts Landing, King Ferry, Schodack Landing, Webster Crossing, Wells Bridge
NORTH CAROLINA: Sneads Ferry
NORTH DAKOTA: Churchs Ferry
OHIO: Martins Ferry
PENNSYLVANIA: Chadds Ford, Dingmans Ferry, Rices Landing, Smiths Ferry, Washington Crossing
SOUTH CAROLINA: Galivants Ferry
VIRGINIA: Davis Wharf, Jenkins Bridge, Seven Mile Ford
WASHINGTON: Copalis Crossing
WEST VIRGINIA: Gallipolis Ferry, Gauley Bridge, Harpers Ferry

Naming towns and villages after the local private commerce center was simple for the early namers, but there was more, much more, they could do to give character and identity to their communities.

Breaking with Tradition

The early colonists and pioneers had a great deal of freedom in the naming of their homes and neighborhoods. There were neither rules nor regulations to stop them from placing the most outlandish name on a stretch of land, a body of water, or a lofty peak.

The early New Englanders were quite conservative. They transplanted names from their native homes to their adopted homes. Later, when men and women had been nurtured by the wild soil of the New World, they would not allow themselves to be hampered by ironclad tradition. They were creating custom and tradition of their own. The uniqueness of their experience caused them to fabricate unusual names and leave little or no record as to why. Some of these names bedevil and becloud the curious of today.

The names do not always mean what they say . . . as the reader will soon find out.

ALABAMA

Coffee Springs, Sunny South

ALASKA

Chicken, Red Devil

CHICKEN—This town was named about 1895, during the Alaskan gold rush. The name probably was obtained from the nearby

Chicken Creek, called that by prospectors when they found the least amount of gold at the bottom amid the greatest amount of gravel. The creek produced, in their language, "chicken pay gold."

ARIZONA

Bumble Bee, Happy Jack, Show Low, Snowflake

SHOW LOW—Two pioneers, Marion Clark and Corydon Cooley, decided to split up and dissolve their partnership. They decided to play a game called Seven-Up, with the low card winning. When Clark demanded that his partner "show low," Cooley pulled a deuce—and won the townsite. The main street of Show Low was originally called Deuce of Clubs.

ARKANSAS

Hon, Oil Trough, Okay, Romance, Sweet Home, Umpire

SWEET HOME—Slaves named this town after they completed building a church.

CALIFORNIA

Happy Camp, Likely, Rough and Ready, Standard, Whiskeytown

WHISKEYTOWN—This town took its name from the Whiskey Creek. A mule team was carrying a supply of spirits when something happened—one of the loads shifted and kegs of whiskey tumbled into the stream, floating near the townsite. Regarding this accident as an act of God, the residents decided that was the name they wanted. Postal officials, however, balked at the notion and refused. The townspeople fought for what they believed in until 1952, when they got the name they always wanted—Whiskeytown!

COLORADO

Climax, Hygiene, Marvel, Model, Rye, Yellow Jacket

YELLOW JACKET—This name came from the nearby Yellow Jacket Canyon, which had been named for "Old Chief Yellowjacket, a mean old skunk" and chief of the Navahos.

FLORIDA

Christmas, Goldenrod, Land O'Lakes, Panacea

GOLDENROD—This town was first called Gabriel, then Suburban Heights. The residents felt that both names were too sophisticated for their locale. Finally, they agreed to name it after the local "stink weed" that blanketed the area.

GEORGIA

Climax, Social Circle, Talking Rock

CLIMAX—This town is situated at the high point between Dothan, Alabama, and Waycross, Georgia. Engineers named it Climax while surveying for the Atlantic Coast Line Railroad.

IDAHO

Dingle, Headquarters

HEADQUARTERS—The Potlatch Forests, Inc., used this place as the center for their operations.

INDIANA

Advance, Converse, French Lick, Onward, Roachdale

FRENCH LICK—The original title was The Lick, because animals would come to the area to lick the moisture off the wet rocks. In the early nineteenth century, French settlers erected a fort on the site as protection against the Indians. Ergo, the alteration in name.

IOWA

Hardy, Soldier

KANSAS

Admire, Agenda, Coats, Home, Protection, Radium, Rice

KENTUCKY

Ages, Busy, Chance, Climax, Cranks, Dwarf, Fisty, Halo

DWARF—About 1883, this town was named for an early settler of short stature, "Short Jerry" Combs.

LOUISIANA

Alto, Belcher, Book, Cut Off, Dry Prong, Iota, Many, Plain Dealing

DRY PRONG—The Big Creek in Louisiana is formed by two streams. In the late nineteenth century, a family attempted to construct a waterwheel on one of these streams. Arriving in winter, they found their stream filled with water, but before they could begin work, it was summer and the waterway had dried up. To their chagrin, they learned they owned land on the "dry prong" of the creek.
The name was adopted in 1906.

MARYLAND

Accident, Fair Play, Secretary

SECRETARY—This site was named for Lord Baltimore's secretary, who built "My Lady Shewell" manor there in 1667.

MICHIGAN

Covert, Les Cheneaux Club, Maybee

MINNESOTA

Climax, Embarrass, Pillager, Tenstrike

TENSTRIKE—Homesteaders in the 1890's were forced to row from the railroad terminus to this spot to settle their claims. Im-

CHUG!
CHUG!
CHUG!

pressed with the beauty of the area, one man said: "I think we've made a ten-strike." The term comes from the game of tenpins, an early form of bowling.

MISSISSIPPI

Bobo, Learned, Money, Soso

SOSO—A visitor to the local store always responded to questions about the state of his health with the comment: "So so." When a post office was to be established in the town—and a name was needed—the townspeople felt that his comment best expressed the sentiments of the community.

MISSOURI

Boss, Foil, Half Way, Huzzah, Licking, Tiff

MONTANA

Emigrant, Intake, Locate, Power, Pray

NEBRASKA

Colon, Friend, Funk, Surprise

FRIEND—Not from any feeling of comradeship did this town derive its name. It reflected the family name, Friend, of one of the principal landowners.

NEVADA

Jackpot

NEW MEXICO

Dusty, House, Loving, Organ, Pep, Truth or Consequences

TRUTH OR CONSEQUENCES—Formerly called Hot Springs, this community voted to change its name for the commercial advantages available through a then-popular radio program.

NEW YORK

Climax, Neversink, Painted Post

PAINTED POST—The Indians called the site *Tecarnasetea-ah,* which meant "a hewn sign." A 1780 account reveals that an Indian chief won a great victory there, during which he had killed twenty-eight of the enemy. To commemorate this event, he had a monument erected—a squared-off tree, painted red, with the headless figures of the dead emblazoned in black.

NORTH CAROLINA

Cashiers, Climax, Husk, Relief, Salvo, Toast

NORTH DAKOTA

Cando, Heil

OHIO

Charm, Dart, Gore, Gratis, Put-in-Bay

PUT-IN-BAY—The name for this particular town is allegedly taken from the words of Commodore Oliver Hazard Perry after the battle of Lake Erie: "Put the ships in the bay."

OKLAHOMA

Bowlegs, Bromide, Cement, Page, Slick

BOWLEGS—This place commemorates Seminole Chief "Billy Bowlegs," who, together with his entire family, was killed in an Indian feud.

OREGON

Boring, Bridal Veil, Drain, Friend, Riddle, Sixes, Talent

SIXES—Though gambling with dice played a role in the life of the pioneer, it had nothing to do with the town name Sixes. This town derived its name from the Indian phrase *Klahowya Sikhs,* the Chinook equivalent of "Peace be with you."

PENNSYLVANIA

Brave, Home, Intercourse, Light Street, Needmore, Pillow, Transfer

INTERCOURSE—The original town was called Cross Keys, after the signboard of a local tavern that operated there in 1754. The name was changed in 1813 because of its commercial location on a prosperous crossroads.

SOUTH CAROLINA

Coward, Round O

SOUTH DAKOTA

Tea

TEA—This name was selected by the townspeople simply because it was short.

TENNESSEE

Crump, Guys, Reverie, Static

STATIC—In the early days of wireless telegraphy, static waves were called "strays" or "X's." The town of Static is located on an important crossroads or "X-roads."

TEXAS

Ace, Art, Best, Blanket, Coat, Coy City, Dime Box, Grit, Guy, Rule, Satin, Seven Sisters, Spade, Telegraph, Telephone

ACE—Not named for the high card in a deck of cards, this town honors the memory of an early settler, Ace Emmanual.

UTAH

Dutch John, Price

DUTCH JOHN—Established as a town in 1959, it was named for John Hunslinger, a German horsetrader who lived in the area during the 1800's.

VERMONT

North Hero, South Hero

VIRGINIA

Bee, Breaks, Cash, Chance, Handsom, Index, Modest Town, Pound

BEE—Confederate General Barnard E. Bee, who is supposed to have supplied General Thomas J. Jackson with his nickname, "Stonewall," is commemorated in this town name.

WASHINGTON

Black Diamond, Index

WEST VIRGINIA

Bud, Dink, Given, Left Hand, Man, Nitro, Odd, Pie, Rig, Romance, Thursday, War

ODD—When the townspeople got around to naming their town in 1868, they wanted something truly distinctive to set them apart from towns and cities throughout the state. So they chose the name "Odd."

THURSDAY—While filling out the proper government forms, a town official goofed and wrote the day of the week in the space specified for the name of the community.

WISCONSIN

Arena, Chili, Hustler, Pence, Siren

CHILI—Crews were sent by the railroad to paint a station sign at the town of Cedarhurst. They arrived in January. Faced with a temperature of 47 degrees below zero, they decided to paint the sign to reflect the climate and how it affected them—complete with their own brand of spelling.

WYOMING

Chugwater, Linch

CHUGWATER—The name is borrowed from the Chugwater River. The Indians called the spot "the river at the place where the buffalo chug." "Chug" was their way of describing the sound the animals made when they drank.

There are countless other villages, towns, and cities that reflect the devil-may-care attitude of pioneering namers. These are just a small sample.

11

Do You Really Want to Know?

You've read this far, and your city or town wasn't mentioned. You feel offended. Yet, at the same time, your curiosity has reached the point where all you care about is finding out more about the name. And, you're going to do your own detective work.

Before people begin to dig for the roots of a name, they must have some idea how far they are prepared to go. If the ground rules are not set up beforehand, the investigation can become endless and very boring.

Ask yourself first how much you really want to know. Do you just want to satisfy that gnawing curiosity, or do you want to delve deeply into the reasons why and who?

After you've answered those questions, you're ready to proceed.

If you decide to dig deeply, prepare yourself to devote a great deal of time and energy before you arrive at your final answer. You must also be aware that good research always involves the frustrations of seeming dead ends and false turns. Don't let them get you down! The solution is well worth the struggle.

Now, where do you begin?

Let's start with place names.

For the past hundred or more years, amateur and professional name detectives have tried to compile accurate lists of names from across the nation, with the derivation of the various names. Despite the searchers' enthusiasm and talent, there are hundreds, perhaps thousands, of name sources that have not yet been deciphered completely.

Their work is available for your benefit. Good investigation is very much like a strongly constructed building. It must have a good foundation, good supports, and fit into the general scheme of things. Only when this is complete can the decorative details be added. In other words, you must start at the bottom and work your way up.

Using other persons' data will help reduce the total amount of time you must devote to your study.

Many place names can be found in standard local, county, and state histories. After this nation's Centennial in 1876, many such books were published as a contribution to future knowledge. Some are quite valuable, others are nothing more than promotional publications to honor the persons who contributed money to have the books published. It will be up to you to judge the value and accuracy of the individual works. The same is true of volumes that were produced before the Bicentennial. To check your sources, compare three books or papers. If they agree, they may be correct. But look in the acknowledgments section or in the bibliography at the back of each book to be sure that the authors of your three sources did not use the same authority themselves!

After you have found a reference book, consult the index. If the name you want appears there, take a 3″ × 5″ index card and copy the information word for word onto it. At the top left-hand corner of the card, type or print the name of the place about which you are seeking information. On the right, identify the source material: author, title, page numbers. Don't add or subtract from the published words. Later, when you decide to write about the name, you will rephrase the quotation, but not before. Original quotations, in moderation, will add spice to the writings you produce.

When you have finished with the first book, go on to the next . . . and the next . . . and the next. Keep a record of all your sources. A separate set of index cards should be maintained as a bibliography. Within a very short time you will have piled up a small collection of sources that mention your particular place name.

Before you set aside each book, look in the bibliographic section or in the list of sources, if one is printed in the back of the book. Many of the early regional histories lack this material. The reason is quite simple. Many early researchers had a luxury that today's writer lacks—they could tap the thoughts, words, and memories of many of the early settlers and pioneers.

If you are lucky enough to find a reading list, look through it carefully to see if any other books are noted that deal with your area of study. If they do, write down the complete information: author, title, place of publication, publisher, and date. Consult the card catalog in the library for those books. If you find them, write down the catalog numbers. Search for the books in the section listed, then pore through them. If they are not on the shelf, ask the librarian to obtain them from the stacks for you. It is possible, even then, that the books will not surface. Many times, rare and valuable—and some not so rare—volumes disappear without a trace, because some selfish, unthinking individuals borrowed the books —permanently.

But that is not the end of the line. Many books are available through interlibrary loan. You might have to wait a week or two, but getting the books might be well worth the delay.

When you get your new volume, consult its index and proceed as you did before, keeping cards on all information.

You might want to read what precedes and what follows the text reference to your subject. Often the authors build up to the place name with facts about the events that led up to the founding or naming. This is very important if you want to develop as complete a story as possible.

Another starting point are the Federal Writers Project volumes on place-naming. They can be found in most libraries. The facts these books present, unfortunately, must be taken with a grain of salt. Some of the derivations are made-up—not actual—name sources. Better, in most respects, is Stewart's *American Place-Names*. Though Stewart's work contains thousands of names, it is only a selection.

Since you can do most of your basic investigation at your local library branch, take the time to talk with the librarians on the staff to learn what assistance they can offer and what books are actually available. The librarians will be glad to save you time and trouble by steering you in the right direction.

Most libraries also have map collections. The map librarian takes pride in the collecting of local maps and geographic drawings of the area. If you look at these charts carefully, you may find the information you need—in the form of a land grant or the name of an owner of a particular plot of ground. In addition, a map that shows the way an area looked might possibly tell you why a town was called by the name of a hill or a stand of trees.

A good idea is to get a modern road map of the area you want to study. Be sure the map is disposable and not one of a kind. Cut out the section that deals with your research. An excellent rule is to center your place on the map, then, using a compass, circle an area of ten to twenty miles in diameter. Paste this section down on an 8½″ × 11″ sheet of plain paper. You can use this as a guide when you study the old maps.

Using the modern map, look at the earlier renderings. See if you can find landmarks or bodies of water that haven't changed over the years. By locating them, you can relate the present to the past.

Again, using your index cards, note the source and the date of the map and write down your observations. File them away with your other cards, under the proper subject name.

In many larger cities and towns, there are offices where deeds and land surveys are deposited. These are available for study by the public. In smaller locales, such records are usually stored in a county office.

These are the next records you will want to inspect. Survey maps and drawings will probably show you the changes in the boundary lines between what now exists and what was once there. This information is important, because city limits and town boundaries might have shifted over the years. And if your town was the result of the incorporation of several villages, you might find there is more history about it than you originally expected.

Many city and county offices will also make photocopies of the records available to you for a small fee. If you can afford these copies—always ask the price before you tell them to go ahead—they will provide you with illustrations for your project. Besides, you can examine the copies for new clues at your leisure.

Before the new, streamlined postal system in this nation, the local postmaster was a valuable source of information on place

names. This devoted servant of the public kept standard letters on file with which to respond to queries about how that particular post office got its name. Though you can't count on that type of service today, it is still worth a try. All you have to lose is the postage.

When you write to the postmaster, ask specific questions: When was the post office opened? Who was the first postmaster? What was the official name at that time, and was there another name before that?

If you find there was an earlier name, you should go back to your county histories and look in the index for information on the earlier name. The date of change is your guide. If the history book was published before that date, the reference will be to the earlier name.

When writing to anyone for information, have the courtesy to include a self-addressed, stamped envelope. People—regardless of their position or station in life—respond quickly when the writer does this. In fact, human nature being what it is, the person feels obligated to respond, because you've expended some money in your search.

Any information obtained from a postmaster should be added to your card file together with the source. List it as "letter from 'name of postmaster' to 'your name' and date."

After doing all this, you will probably have a good idea about the source of the name and the date of settlement or incorporation.

You can stop at this point and feel content that you have accomplished what you set out to do. But curiosity is a strange and wonderful thing. You might decide that you still want to know more about the person or the event behind the name. This is where the ambitious detectives are separated from their less-curious counterparts.

You know the name and the date. How do you find out more?

If the source was a person, refer back to your county or city history books. Look in the index for that person's name and follow the same procedure as you did on the naming: complete a card file of background on that individual's deeds and accomplishments. Add this to your information bank.

Look in *Who's Who* and *Who Was Who* for additional personal clues. While you are paging through these volumes, you might want to hunt up references to your own family name. You could be surprised to learn that some distant ancestor had a role in the founding of your own hometown.

Two other valuable reference sources, which people often neglect, are the dictionary and the encyclopedia. *The Random House Dictionary of the English Language* and *The Random House Encyclopedia* are both excellent.

The *Encyclopaedia Britannica* offers the most facts, but you may have a hard time finding your way through the wealth of detail.

Historical societies of the city, county, and state have, over the years, gathered a considerable amount of material on people, places, and things. A visit to the headquarters of your local historical society should provide some exciting facts.

When you have exhausted your library sources, you can begin a letter-writing campaign to get more information.

If the person for whom your place was named was involved in military activity, you can write to the National Archives, Old Army and Navy Records, in Washington, D.C. Request the forms needed to acquire land records or military service files on your person. The staff at the Archives are very cooperative and will research the person for you. If they locate information, they will charge you a small amount for photocopying all the information they found in the files. If, on the other hand, their search is fruitless, there will be no charge for the time involved. This is one of the most inexpensive and valuable services provided by the National Archives.

Other sources of facts on military figures can be obtained through your local library in such books as Boatner's *Encyclopedia of the American Revolution;* Heitman's *Historical Register of Officers of the Continental Army;* Cullem's *Biographical Register of the Officers and Graduates of the United States Military Academy at West Point, N.Y., Since Its Establishment in 1802;* and the *Official Army Register,* published by the U.S. Adjutant General's Office.

There are many figures for whom places were named who had

little or no military involvement. The *Dictionary of American Biography,* the *New York Times Index,* and *Who's Who* will help with these.

Newspapers, though sometimes unreliable in reporting true facts on place-naming, are another source of clues on people and places. Some newspapers even publish a more-or-less regular column on place names and street names. Though leaning heavily on folklore in some instances, they can be used to check against other sources.

Only through maturity and experience will you be able to separate truth from fallacy in the newspaper clippings. Too often, reporters—in their haste to meet deadlines—refer only to past newspaper clips and accept them as fact. In so doing, they perpetuate myths. You have to be extremely careful about your use of this information.

You can get substantial information and leads to other sources on both active and abandoned military posts by writing to the Center for Military History, Department of the Army, Washington, D.C.; *Army* (or *Navy*) *Times* magazine, if the installation is still in active operation, or, if it is decommissioned, to the Council on Abandoned Military Posts, U.S.A., Arlington, Virginia.

Research is lonely. Each "detective" feels that he or she is working alone. This is not the case. There are thousands of people in the world who are interested in the same subject as you. Some of them have joined the American Name Society and are more than willing to share with you the results of their own labors. A letter to the Society will open many doors you might not have known existed. Another helpful group is the American Association for State and Local History.

This is all well and good for the study of place names. What do you do if you want to know more about street, road, and highway names?

Thoroughfares are a little more difficult to research because in most cases no records were ever kept as to why a particular name was selected or used.

That lack of planning on the part of city and town officials should not stop you from delving into the subject.

Use the same methods you used when you were digging up the story of a particular town name. Also, you should make a stop at the road records department in your municipality. If one does not exist under that name, try the district highway engineering office. In either place you will find the engineering drawings, site plans, dates of dedication, and other relevant information on roadways.

A careful study of that data will provide you with a specific date, and sometimes a notation that a particular roadway or path went through someone's property. If you are lucky, you might find that the current name is the same as that property owner's.

With the date when the street was opened or dedicated, you will have a starting point. If the thoroughfare bears the name of a person or an event, you can be sure that the individual lived, or the event took place, before or during the time of the street-naming. A look through the local or county history books or the local newspaper files will then be in order. Most times, you will be able to make a careful guess as to the true source of the name.

Other times, you will be able to determine that the roadway led somewhere, such as to a church, a meetinghouse, a school. This object might be the source of the name, even though the route of the road has been altered over the years. Follow the same record-keeping procedure after you have isolated the name source as you did with place names.

Now that you have filled several cardboard boxes with index cards and have absorbed so much information, what are you going to do with it?

Sharing Knowledge

With all the facts you have gathered, you can now outline your material and get ready to write a complete story on what you have discovered.

Take all your index cards and put them into some kind of order. The most helpful order for either place names or street names should be by date or approximate time, starting from before the town or the street existed. Next comes your material on the founding or the dedication; then the changes that took place—either in the name or in the boundaries—and finally today's descriptions and details. Sprinkle through the story—when they apply—personal quotations or stories that will make the account more enjoyable to a reader. Most writers seem to forget they are readers first and then, with skill and practice, become writers. What most appeals to you as a reader should be what you include in your writing.

History can be a very boring subject if it is treated as a dry recital of dates and facts. Too many books on history lie under a mound of dust in our nation's libraries because writers forgot that their works were intended to be read.

Don't be one of these individuals. Make the mix of those little-known facts an important part of your outline.

After you have completed your outline, read over your cards again. Ask yourself questions that you think a reader might ask. Why did so-and-so settle in this particular area and not in some other? Where did he live before? What happened to the rest of his family? Why was a particular roadway cut through a forest so that

the road looks like a serpentine? If you find, in the course of your personal interrogation, that you've left some stones unturned, go back to your original material and dig some more until all the questions that you might ask another writer are answered fully.

If you followed instructions carefully, and copied down source material word for word, you will now have the chance to change them to your own words. Don't use the other person's exact words. Plagiarism is a common crime with beginning writers. Though it is flattering to the author whose work has been stolen, it does nothing to improve the skills of the new writer.

Quotations from manuscripts, books, and documents should be reduced, as far as possible, to today's language. The original quotations should be used only as pithy remarks that add color and flavor to your story. A good rule to remember is never to quote anything that you can say better yourself, and, conversely, never rephrase another's words when those words say it better than you.

With your outline and your cards, you're now ready to write. Good luck!

Oh, one more thing: document each piece of evidence by noting the source. Don't leave anything to memory. Check it out.

Your project is now completed and you're satisfied that it's a good piece of detective work and writing. Where do you go from here?

This is the moment when you are ready to share your discoveries with others. By taking what you did and offering it to others you will help them to increase their knowledge, just as you have done, and, perhaps, build upon your foundation.

First share your story with the teacher, then with the rest of the class. If the teacher is pleased with your work, a similar project—a bigger one—might be started for the entire class. If this is the case, the classroom will be the first public exhibition of your work.

Why stop with one class?

If the teacher has no objection, the whole story might be photocopied or mimeographed for distribution to the entire student body. That is good exposure for the work you've done, and it might prompt others to try their hand at the naming game.

What else can you do?

You should take copies to the local library and to the historical society and ask to have them put on file. Curious generations of the future will then be able to refer to your work and use you as one of their references.

The American Name Society will also be interested in having a copy of your research report, and they will distribute that information to all the members of the group.

If the librarian and the historical society think you have done a good job, you might want to present a copy of your story to a local church, social, or civic group to print and sell during their fund-raising drive.

Local newspapers, both daily and weekly, are always on the lookout for small space fillers of local interest. You might want to divide your report into smaller articles and submit them to the editor. Be sure to look over the newspaper before you rewrite your material. Check what size articles are usually run—this will help you gauge the length.

Don't expect to receive a great deal of money for your first article. Small newspapers, the best market for your efforts, usually pay starting writers with a few dollars at best, or a few free copies of the newspaper at worst. If the material is acceptable and accepted, don't worry about the money. In some ways it is better to have a by-lined article in a newspaper than to receive a small sum of cash.

Your class or club might want to try a full-scale investigation of your city, if it's a large one, your county or state, or your section of the country.

Even if you never publish the results of your detective work in a newspaper, magazine, or book, think what you have gained.

You have delved into the past and come up with some understanding of what makes people tick. There are many people in this world who, despite age and maturity, have never uncovered an inkling of what you have learned.

Besides the obvious enjoyment you had, think of the subjects you have explored.

You've learned a little bit of French, German, Spanish—even Middle English. You've touched on geography and geology.

You've studied genealogy, political science, government relations, land expansion, psychology, and sociology.

You've had a liberal arts course—maybe even on the college level—and you never even knew it!

Bibliography

The following list of references is a selection of the better sources available to persons interested in researching the derivation of place and street names.

Alotta, Robert I. *Street Names of Philadelphia.* Temple University Press, 1975.

American Historical Review. Washington, D.C.: American Historical Association, 1895 to date.

Army Times. Guide to Army Posts. 2d ed. Stackpole Co., 1966.

Bacheller, Martin A., ed. *The CBS News Almanac.* Hammond Almanac, 1977.

Bibliographic Index: A Cumulative Bibliography of Bibliographies. H. W. Wilson Co., 1937 to date.

Biography Index: A Cumulative Index to Biographical Material in Books and Magazines. H. W. Wilson Co., 1946 to date.

Boatner, Mark M. *The Civil War Dictionary.* David McKay Co., 1959.

———*Encyclopedia of the American Revolution.* Rev. ed. David McKay Co., 1974.

Center of Military History. Norman Miller Cary, Jr., comp. *Guide to U.S. Army Museums and Historic Sites.* U.S. Government Printing Office, 1975.

Cumming, John. *A Guide for the Writing of Local History.* Michigan American Revolution Bicentennial Commission, 1974.

Dictionary of American Biography. 20 vols., index, and 4 supplement vols. Charles Scribner's Sons, 1928–1974.

Donehoo, Dr. George P. *A History of the Indian Villages and Place Names in Pennsylvania.* Harrisburg: Telegraph Press, 1928.

Encyclopaedia Britannica. Encyclopaedia Britannica, Inc., 1974.

Espenshade, A. Howry. *Pennsylvania Place Names.* 1925. Gale Research Company, 1969 reprint ed.

Harrington, Mark Raymond. *The Indians of New Jersey.* 1938. Rutgers University Press, 1963.

Heckewelder, John. *History, Manners, and Customs of the Indian Nations Who Once Inhabited Pennsylvania and the Neighboring States.* 1819. Arno Press, 1971 reprint ed.

Heitman, Francis Bernard. *Historical Register and Dictionary of the United States Army, From Its Organization, Sept. 29, 1789, to March 2, 1903.* 2 vols. University of Illinois Press, 1965 reprint ed.

Journal of American History. Bloomington, Ind.: Organizaton of American Historians, 1914 to date.

Leach, Douglas Edward. *The Northern Colonial Frontier, 1607–1763.* Holt, Rinehart & Winston, 1966.

Long, E. B., and Long, Barbara. *The Civil War Day by Day: An Almanac, 1861–1865.* Doubleday & Co., 1971.

Lynch, Thomas Montgomery, ed. *Encyclopedia of Pennsylvania Biography.* Lewis Historical Publishing Co., 1923.

McMahon, William. *South Jersey Towns: History and Legend.* Rutgers University Press, 1973.

Mitchell, James, ed. *The Random House Encyclopedia.* Random House, 1977.

Moyer, Armond and Winfred, comps. *The Origins of Unusual Place-Names.* Keystone Publishing Associates, 1958.

Murray, Robert A. *Brief Guide to Research on Army Posts.* Washington, D.C.: Council on Abandoned Military Posts, 1969.

Names. Potsdam, N.Y.: State University College, 1953 to date.

New York Times Index, The. Sept. 1851–1905, Jan. 1911 to date.

New York Times Obituaries Index 1858–1968, The. New York Times Co., 1970.

Parker, Donald Dean. *Local History: How to Gather It, Write It and Publish It.* Rev. and ed. by Bertha E. Josephson. New York: Social Science Research Council, 1944.

Philadelphia Bibliography Center. *Union List of Microfilms: A Basic List of Holdings in the United States and Canada.* Philadelphia, 1961.

Poulton, Helen J. *The Historian's Handbook: A Descriptive Guide to Reference Works.* University of Oklahoma Press, 1972.

Prucha, Francis Paul. *A Guide to the Military Posts of the United States, 1789–1895.* State Historical Society of Wisconsin, 1964.

Quimby, Myron J. *Scratch Ankle, U.S.A.: American Place Names and Their Derivation.* A. S. Barnes & Co., 1969.

Rouse, Parke, Jr. *The Great Wagon Road: From Philadelphia to the South.* McGraw-Hill Book Co., 1973.

Scharf, J. Thomas, and Westcott, Thompson. *History of Philadelphia, 1609–1884,* 3 vols. Philadelphia: L. H. Evarts & Co., 1884. AMS Press, 1976 reprint ed.

Scott, John Anthony. *Settlers on the Eastern Shore, 1607–1750.* Alfred A. Knopf, 1967.

Sheehy, Eugene P. *Guide to Reference Books.* 9th ed. American Library Association, 1976.

Stein, Jess, ed. *The Random House Dictionary of the English Language.* Random House, 1966.

Stewart, George R. *American Place-Names.* Oxford University Press, 1970.

————*Names on the Land: A Historical Account of Place-Naming in the United States.* Houghton Mifflin Co., 1967.

U.S. Postal Service. *1978 National Zip Code Directory.* U.S. Government Printing Office, 1977.

U.S. War Department. *Atlases to Accompany the Official Records of the Union and Confederate Armies.* 3 vols. U.S. Government Printing Office, 1891–1895.

Weslager, C. A. *The English on the Delaware: 1610–1682.* Rutgers University Press, 1967.

Wildes, Harry Emerson. *The Delaware* (Rivers of America). Farrar & Rinehart, 1940.

In addition to these works, the interested researcher will find countless works on individual states, cities, and towns in the card catalog at the local library. Articles on the subject also appear in historical journals published by state and local organizations.

Specific information can also be obtained by writing to any of the following organizations:

American Name Society, c/o The State University College, Potsdam, NY 13676. (This organization can supply you with a list of the state directors of the Place Name Survey of the United States.)

Council on Abandoned Military Posts, U.S.A., P.O. Box 171, Arlington, VA 22210

Domestic Geographic Names, U.S. Board on Geographic Names, Defense Mapping Agency, Building 56, U.S. Naval Observatory, Washington, DC 20305

National Archives, Old Army and Navy Records (Military Service Records, Land Bounty Records and Pension Claims), 8th Street and Pennsylvania Avenue, Washington, DC 20408

Library, U.S. Military Academy, West Point, NY 10996

Acknowledgments

The germ of the idea for this book began one day in the spring of 1978 when I was asked to talk to students at Philadelphia's Cook-Wissahickon School. Miss Carole Millendorf, the school librarian, wanted me to explain to her students how I got to know so much about Philadelphia street names.

What began as a recitation of names rapidly turned into a heated question and answer period on how I researched the names, where I found my material, and why I selected certain ones and not others. I spoke to two classes that day—and walked away exhausted. Those students had dug deeply into my consciousness and made me tell them the tricks of the naming game. Later I learned there was method in their madness: they had taken on a class project to research the names of their streets and neighborhoods. I was had—and didn't even know it!

The experience there started me thinking—and talking.

Nancy Over, a former Westminster staffer, heard me. She also read some of my vignettes, published in the *Ambler Gazette*, *Today's Post*, and *The Springfield Sun*. Do a book, she said. I did, Nance . . . and here it is.

Having an idea and being able to put it into words which ultimately end up on the printed page are two entirely different things. I have been supported and inspired by a lot of people. Most of their names, however, disappear when I sit down at the typewriter.

Jerry Post, of the Free Library of Philadelphia, is a good friend who kept after me to look at countless maps in the library's collection. Without realizing it, he had given me a small portion of his great love—and a smattering of his prodigious knowledge—of maps and map interpretation. His co-worker at the Free Library, Joe DeNuccio, can't be forgotten either. Joe bailed me out at the eleventh hour when the manuscript deadline was advanced two months.

Last, but not least, the help, advice, and friendship of Bro. Patrick Ellis, F.S.C., president of LaSalle College, must be acknowledged. Without him, I never would have had the peace, privacy, and quiet that was necessary to create this book. The environment at LaSalle is most conducive to scholarly work. It's really a shame I didn't realize that when I was an undergraduate.

There are people I have neglected to mention. They know who they are . . . and I'm sorry that I forgot.

Geographic Index

General Index